Unexpected
GLORY

The remarkable story of
encountering God's mercy
in unexpected places.

By
Teresa Brownlee

All For The Glory of God !

Unexpected Glory

The remarkable story of encountering
God's mercy in unexpected places.

ISBN-13: 978-1503358690
ISBN-10: 1503358690

Author: Teresa Brownlee

For permission or other inquiries, go to:

www.UnexpectedGlory.com

Scripture references are from the New American Bible (NAB).

Some names and places have been changed to protect their identities.

Ron and Judy Miller: Benefactors

Editor, Counselor, and Production Manager: Linda Maria

Book design and layout: David S. Larson.

Cover illustration: by Cathie Norris.

Printed as a work of non-fiction in the United States of America.

CONTENTS

Preface i

Acknowledgment v

Glory One The Glory Seeds 1

Glory Two The Stirring of My Memory 11

Glory Three Miracle at the Truck Stop 19

Glory Four Sprinting to the Church 27

Glory Five The Upper Room 33

Glory Six The Pardon Prayer 41

Glory Seven The Rising Catholics 47

Glory Eight Santa Maria Beckons 54

Glory Nine All that Glitters is Gold 62

Glory Ten Medjugorje Knockout! 76

Glory Eleven From Grateful Dead to Diaper Head 85

Glory Twelve Born Again in Water 94

Glory Thirteen Queen of Liberation 105

Glory Fourteen Good Friday Blindside 113

Glory Fifteen Saint Anthony and the Tomatoes 128

Glory Sixteen God's Drive-Thru Order 136

Glory Seventeen Mystery Billboard at Circle K 145

Glory Eighteen Divine Mercy at the Jordan River 155

Glory Nineteen A Butterfly in My Life 169

Glory Twenty	The Lamb and the Wedding	181
Glory Twenty-One	Moses and the Blessed Sacrament	190
Glory Twenty-Two	Jesus, I'll Work for You!	199
Glory Twenty-Three	The Magnificent Magnificat Meal	208
Glory Twenty-Four	The Passover and the Crucifix	218
Glory Twenty-Five	Is This What I Was Born For?	230
Glory Twenty-Six	The Praetorium	237
Glory Twenty-Seven	The Flowers of Saint Francis	245
Glory Twenty-Eight	Mirianna and Divine Mercy	254
Glory Twenty-Nine	Something Beautiful for God	268
Glory Thirty	Forgiveness – The Key to God's Heart	277
Glory Thirty-One	Priests for Lifers	287
	Epilogue	301

And ALL the Glory Be to God!

PREFACE

I will not fully understand God's Sweeping Hand forming His plan for a soul, until I am with Him. But I will try to acknowledge the wind of the Holy Spirit moving in my life, a life that would culminate into a dramatic miraculous conversion almost a half century later. I send all my love to Mother Cabrini and her sisters, as I began my journey at age two with their order in Los Angeles, California.

After the Cabrini sisters left Los Angeles, I was placed at the Little Flower Missionary House in Los Angeles with the Carmelites. When you are knee high to a grasshopper and at eye level everyday with a captivating Crucifix and Rosary that imagery imprints upon your soul. For the rest of my life, when I see a Carmelite in a brown habit with a Rosary hanging down, I feel like I am home. My life began with the Carmelites when I was still only two years old. They fostered a great love for God in me which required much prayer and attention. They cared for me as their very own daughter. The Carmelites are my earliest Catholic memories. May The Lord bless them always.

At age seven, I entered Saint Thomas the Apostle School in Los Angeles, California. I became a student of the Sisters of the Immaculate Heart of Mary and had the best beginning in elementary school possible. The nuns watched me fastidiously on the playground, caring for me in the hallways, and in the classroom, as I was all over the place. I can only say that all I remember is kindness from the Sisters and Reverend Monsignor John Gallagher on a daily basis. I have really gone deep into my memory and recognize the wonderful effort they all made to give me a powerful beginning in schooling and in the faith! The Great Church of Saint Thomas on Pico Boulevard in Los Angeles is one of my most favorite memories as a child. Walking with Sister to Mass with the students and learning all our prayers was a strong part of my formation.

St. Thomas the Apostle Church ministers to 10,000 families of various ethnic backgrounds today. It is one of the most heavily populated areas in the United States and is the beacon, the light, for thousands of families to be fed with God's Word and His Holy Eucharist. At this time in history, I am compelled to write this book to share the wonders and miracles that God has bestowed upon me through His Grace emanating from many prayers and concerns of all that had charge of me in the beginning. I am on my face with gratitude to the Lord for placing me in the arms of all those nuns who would play a great role in the transformation of a soul later in life into one who now bleeds Catholic.

May humanity come to understand the gift that is present in the Catholic Education System and in the Catholic Church. Degeneration of veneration is at an all-time high, as well as respect for teachers, parents, and authority. May God please restore what the locusts have eaten!

Thank you Blessed Lord for this incredible gift of access to a living faith.

Our Lady of Mount Carmel, Pray for Us

Ephesians 3:20, 21

To Him be glory in the Church and in Christ Jesus
to all generations, forever and ever. Amen

ACKNOWLEDGMENT

I am looking up to heaven with profound thanksgiving for my parents, godparents, priests and nuns who had charge of my soul when I was very little and also throughout my journey. I am immensely grateful to the Lord God for His Divine Plan for me. He placed me with those who would plant the seeds of Catholicism and cultivate my future with the Church. Those seeds sprouted much later in life into great blossoms of glory!

I also want to thank the Lord for all the special souls that encouraged me through the years to write this book. In particular; Beloved Ron and Judy Miller, the first Catholics on the scene after the Truck Stop Miracle, bringing the Joy of the Lord, as they were always ready to pray me through every challenge, as they are my spiritual Godparents. Elissa Fruciano, who has been a great persistent encourager prodding me on for years to write this book. As contributing editor, she has given clarity to the book as a loving helpmate and fantastic support counselor.

To my precious sister, Linda Maria, an awesome partner in the journey of writing this book, as editor and master formatter, standing by my side through all the trials and tribulations. She worked with me to find the way to get this book to print. The Lord sent her in during the latter stages of this project and she answered His Call. She always worked very hard to keep my voice present. I consider Linda one of the great miracles that took place during the process of publishing this book.

Sekoia Novena Spencer, wonderful soul sister and companion who throughout the years has always reminded me to journalize the miracles. To my beloved friends, Rick and Anna Gibbons, thank you for cheering me on.

I can hear them saying, "We're praying for you, Teresa. We're really excited about this book, hurry up and finish, so we can read it!"

My dear niece, Carol Watkins, phoning me from Austin, Texas, "Aunt Terri, you can do it! I know you can, I am praying for you."

Many, many times she called to encourage me on the journey, as she too knew the hurdles I had to cross in order to write it.

To my reunited friend, Donna Britain, who has helped contribute her English and grammar skills, even during a time of great personal loss, always steadfast with her love and prayers.

I thank all of you from the bottom of my heart. Your unending support for this endeavor is the only reason I finished it before the Lord returns!

My deepest love and gratitude to my incredible daughter, Kimberly, and her amazing husband Robert, for these two have given me some of the greatest chapters in my life. For the love of my life, husband Daniel, of over 49 years, who patiently waited for me to complete this work; his technical assistance has been invaluable to me and his support in the home was that of St. Joseph, a silent and steadfast helpmate.

Thus, I begin a story of God's mercy evident in the Catholic Church and her message of peace which is a spotlight for the entire world. The Lord has always used the littlest ones to bring His Light to the Church. I certainly am little. The precious religious, who had cared for me as a small child, were also little, known only to God. I have been called to write this book to bring glory and honor to the Catholic Church and to the Catholic religious through their contributions that echo throughout all time. The profound and lasting effect that my Catholic Education, the Clergy, the Sisters, and most of all, the Sacraments, have had on my salvation will now be revealed.

ONE

The Glory Seeds Are Sown

I was born in West Los Angeles, California in 1948, in humble surroundings to beautiful, loving parents, Raymond and Lillian. My father was of Spanish descent and my mother was Irish and English. These two loved to ballroom dance and they looked just like movie stars. Our little house on West 17th street in Los Angeles was immaculate and lovely.

Mom and Dad in the 1950s

My mother went to work when I was two years old. I suspect it was the prodding of my paternal grandmother,

Asunción, who was also my Godmother, whispering in my dad's ear where to take me for childcare. I spent several months with the Mother Frances Cabrini Sisters as a toddler. Her mission was always to help immigrants and children. What a blessing for me to be in their care under the influence of Mother Cabrini. The Cabrini sisters did not stay very long in Los Angeles, so my mother had to find another babysitter. They had a great devotion to the Sacred Heart of Jesus.

My grandparents came by ship from Spain to Veracruz, Mexico, where they met. They stayed in Veracruz a couple of years before migrating to the United States. I am sure they were very aware of the Cristiada War and I can only speculate that they knew of Venerable Mother Maria Luisa Josefa, who fled from Mexico with her sisters to Los Angeles, as they were in grave danger during the war. When Mother Luisa first came to Los Angeles, she stayed with the Immaculate Heart of Mary Sisters, whom I was later schooled by – and they were great educators.

In 1929, Mother Luisa would lay the foundation for the future Little Flower Missionary House where I would later begin my journey with the Carmelites as a toddler. Venerable Mother Maria Luisa Josefa of the most Blessed Sacrament would go on to do many heroic acts of charity, schooling, work with the poor and the sick. Hindsight has revealed to me the great blessing I received by being placed in the care of these great women of God as a little one.

My grandparents, Pedro and Asunción, in Veracruz

After my time with the Cabrini Sisters, my mother and father placed me in the Little Flower Missionary House in Los Angeles, developed by Mother Luisa and later managed by her Carmelite order. I believe my parents truly liked these holy babysitters. My mother also needed someone who could keep me for long hours. I can only imagine that during this time I was consecrated to the Sacred Heart of Jesus and the Immaculate Heart of Mary by the Sisters.

My baby book that I mysteriously found one night said, "Little Terri loved praying with the Carmelite nuns and making the Sign of the Cross." All notes in my baby book spoke of the love the Sisters had for me, and it is replete with their comments to my parents of how much I loved to pray with them.

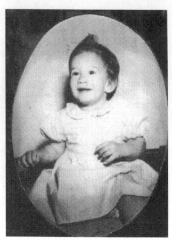

Me at age 2

My favorite Carmelite sisters were Sister Dolores, Sister Conception, Sister Rafael, and Sister Emily. They said I had a wonderful little voice. I thank God that they sang, "Come Holy Spirit," to me, as it came back to me with great power 45 years later. Much of that time, my parents did not have a car, so for a few years, from the age of two, my dad would push me to the Little Flower Nursery School (two miles roundtrip) in an old metal stroller that someone gave them. Dad would do this before and after work.

Little ones walk at their own pace, however, my Dad figured out a way to take charge of the tempo of our walk, so I would be on time. He put me in that old metal stroller they used when I was a baby! My legs were hanging out all over the place. Looking back on it now, their efforts to give me a Catholic education were mysteriously inspired. They worked hard and sacrificed greatly to get me to the Catholic Sisters. The Carmelites would be my extended family for the better part of three years, until I was five – the formative years of a child. There was a public school, Magnolia Elementary, right across the street from our little house. But I only attended that public school for kindergarten. Then came the Holy Spirit guiding my parents once more to take me back to the Sisters.

Beginning in first grade, mom and dad placed me at St. Thomas the Apostle Catholic School and my dad began pushing a lanky six-year old in that same old stroller two miles a day once again. The public school would have been so easy for them. I could have walked it alone as I did for kindergarten. It was literally across the street – you could have thrown a stone at the school from our porch. But my parents made the decision to sacrifice money they did not have, and took great effort to take me to that Blue Ribbon Catholic School. The two years at that school had a profound impact in my life. Mother Superior, Sister De Sales, was my first grade teacher and a great educator.

I provide this background so that it is clear that the probability of this happening was slim-to-none, and the fact that it did was "God inspired." The Holy Spirit was moving in a profound way in my parents' lives, unbeknownst to them.

Unexpected Glory.

My parents were not practicing any religion in the home, and most particularly not Catholicism or Protestantism. Keep that in mind as you read my story.

My parents were not going to Church regularly, only once in a great while. I even struggle to remember any prayer in our home when I was little. The Immaculate Heart of Mary Sisters became my new holy teachers in First Grade at Saint Thomas the Apostle School.

My dad nicknamed me Chapulina, Spanish for grasshopper. I was a very hyperactive kid. The sisters had a hard time just keeping me on the main playground. Sometimes they had to pin me to their habits just to keep me in view, but I kind of enjoyed being next to them. The corporal punishment era often came in the form of strong discipline and strict supervision – but without rulers. They didn't pin me to their side very often, but when they did, I had a feeling of security. I felt loved, protected, and it helped me to learn great respect for my elders because of their appropriately directed discipline.

They taught me everything a good Catholic child should learn: to know, love and serve God; prayer; good penmanship; a love of reading; discipline; love of the Blessed Mother; and all about the Angels and Saints. And, oh, those statues – the Sacred Heart, Our Lady of Fatima, St. Joseph, St. Anthony, Our Lady of Guadalupe, and Glory to God – *The Crucifix* in every classroom. They also had me write, "I will not talk in class, one hundred times!" The battle cry of the nuns was, "Repetition is the best teacher."

As a little girl I found the nuns to be very intriguing. Large rosary beads hanging down one side against their beautiful flowing habits, was only part of the charisma the nuns held for me. My fond memories include: attending Holy Mass before class; the Priest's guidance and serving of the Mass; presenting Our Blessed Mother with a May crown and flowers; and watching the original Fatima movie every year.

My mother and I in Los Angeles

I was seven-years-old when I was presented a high honor award for reading seventy-three books outside of the school curriculum. Monsignor Gallagher, the Pastor, handed it to me on the altar of the Church. This is one example of the special attention that was given to each child at St. Thomas School. Those cherished memories are embedded in my soul.

My parents were not very rooted in the practice of their family faiths; my mother an Irish and English Protestant, and my father a cultural Catholic Spaniard. They were young and distant from those things, so their efforts to procure for me a Catholic surrounding, while they worked, was highly commendable, but a mystery for sure. The grace of God was at work.

Catholic prayers were rarely heard in our home when I was little, and Christian expression was just not visible. No real Catholic ambiance. No Bible readings. I only had a few devout Catholics in my extended family circle who I remember from very early on, but I did not get to spend much time with them growing up. I basically recall more of a Catholic culture, not a living faith.

My beloved parents did not have two pennies to rub together, yet they made a great sacrifice of $25 a month for my schooling at St. Thomas the Apostle School. The amount they paid for the school was as much as they paid for their monthly rent. When I was nine-years-old, we packed and moved to a suburb fifty miles away, and all of the Catholic traditions were left behind, the memories were packed away, and life as I knew it would never be the same.

I would attend Catechism and study for my Confirmation at our new home in La Mirada, California. But the Catholic Church, Catholic School, Clergy, Sisters in Los Angeles, all the Catholic surroundings, that chapter was pretty much closed. I would forget my roots for many, many, years. I don't know why, but it was almost like spiritual amnesia. My continued religious rearing in my La Mirada home paled to the saturation of Catholicism in those early years with the sisters and my Los Angeles Catholic community.

I pray that the Lord unveil this book to all of those loving, wonderful Sisters and Priests, wherever they are in eternity. They were such a marvelous part of my development as a child. I can only say that I never would have become the person I am today, without those seeds of amazing grace planted deeply in my soul. Angels protecting and guiding me, graces from the Lord, and His Sacraments in abundance, perseverance and knowledge were all a part of my Catholic training. Stick-to-itiveness, loving charity and the ability to be a tremendous helpmate were hopefully passed down from my mother, Lillian. Silent strength, an attitude of gratitude with a quiet humility, that I pray were gleaned from my father, Raymond. All my love and thanksgiving goes to my mother, for keeping a historical record called a "baby book," making this testimony possible. Thank you, Lord, for leading me to the hidden baby book, one night after prayer.

Thank you, Lord, for the call upon my parents' hearts to carry out my Catholic education in my early years which they responded to with humility, loving patience and endurance. Thank you, beloved ones, I thank you from the bottom of my heart. The seeds of God's Glory were planted.

Jeremiah 29:11

For I know well the plans
I have in mind for you,
says the Lord, plans for your welfare,
not for your woe!

TWO

The Stirring of My Memory

Well, life was very busy in our new neighborhood. I went on to grow up in a very intense work environment, even going to work at fourteen. By that age, I was also becoming very well trained in playing the piano and I loved it. Although my dad loved to hear me play piano, he was relatively quiet with not much communication going on, but the piano playing was my special time with my father. Both parents worked and taught all three of us girls house cleaning techniques par excellence. They were excellent cooks and owned a restaurant named Ramon's Spanish Kitchen; their specialty was "The Million Dollar Taco."

2010 – A trip back to our home in Los Angeles for me and mom where the seeds of glory were planted.

My parents loved to entertain when they could afford to, serving lots of Mexican food, wine and music. We practiced Catholic "Very Lite" during the next nine years of my life while at home. Once in a while we went to Mass. No real importance was placed on Church, it was mostly for Christmas, Easter or to celebrate a sacrament. I'm grateful to God that I received most of my sacraments with the priests and nuns when growing up in Los Angeles. I received my confirmation at Saint Paul of the Cross Catholic School once we moved to La Mirada. During my confirmation training, I vaguely remember a couple of nuns teaching classes and occasionally the priest, but the faculty were mostly lay teachers. Things had changed over the years. The era of nuns and priests teaching in classrooms was slowly ebbing away.

I soared ahead and became a very self-centered teenager. Spiritual amnesia permeated my life. I attended Catechism, but became increasingly more interested in boys more than anything else. By 16 years of age, I was so headstrong and rebellious that I was not really approachable by my parents anymore. Recalcitrant, independent and losing interest in school, I even lost interest in playing the piano. It must have been very, very upsetting for both my parents.

At 17, I ran off and had a civil marriage to Daniel, a handsome hard-drinking U.S. Marine, freshly back from Vietnam, and I had no idea where that would lead me. We were both in about the same place in terms of our Catholic faith at the time, we were pretty much "checkbox Catholics." God help us! At that time, I received a teaching from my mother which had been passed on to her by her mother, sisters, and personal life experiences. My mother advocated birth control to me. She also made it very clear that when we make mistakes in life it is up to us to clean them up and not to bother other people. So that left an indelible mark on my spirit of, "just handle it."

I was about to learn adult life the hard way. It became a very tumultuous relationship. After seven years of marriage, I was prompted to go to the Catholic Church and begin proceedings for my husband, Dan, and I to marry in the Church. Dan joined me, but only on the day it happened, as he didn't have a connection yet with spiritual matters. The Holy Spirit was guiding me ever so slowly.

I look back in amazement that I pursued the Sacrament of Marriage all alone at 25 years of age. That would be my first real move back towards the Lord. We married in the Church, but still were not attending Mass on Sundays, as my husband liked to go camping on the weekends. I really did not know that I should be going every Sunday because I wasn't raised that way. I did enroll both my children in Catechism though, and was trying to go to Mass occasionally. I seemed to have a very shallow understanding of what it meant to be a practicing Catholic, but the Lord works with us right where we are, and His plans are usually not our plans.

Our lives were full of earning a living and family get-togethers, camping, schooling, etc. There was a lot of drinking going on in our home which spilled over onto our children in a very negative way. There were Vietnam vets coming back from active duty who were friends of my husband, and they would move in for months at a time upon return from war, with a lot of good ol' boy drinking and stories. My little boy Jeff was deeply affected by all of it.

I worked as a waitress for years, and taught piano lessons, anything to help raise the children. I went back to school so that I could help my husband start his modular trailer construction business. I began to take my daughter to Mass more often as I continued to feel a gentle nudge to go. She would get to go to Mass much more than her older brother ever did.

Many years later, when my children were grown, I counseled a dear soul to get an abortion. I did not understand it to be any more than a miscarriage, like I had experienced years before.

This soul was not married, and the fellow she was involved with had a drug and alcohol problem and it seemed like the best thing to do. She called me to ask my advice on her consideration of having an abortion and I led her in that direction, rather than away from it. In the early to middle eighties there was so little press on abortion that the devil could work very well with those not real close to Jesus. I was so positive it was the right thing to do, so pompous and sure footed in my counsel ... after all, just handle it!

After I counseled her, I actually forgot about it and moved on with my life. How horrifying. Years later, my husband and I experienced great difficulties with our children and our business. My son was a businessman on drugs taking a dangerous path. My daughter was now a white Wicca witch on drugs. My husband played video games and drank a lot. I felt pretty helpless in the whole matter. Oh, we were something alright. Then my husband began to get ill and I implored him to close our little construction business and try something else less stressful. How in the world we ever came up with the idea to investigate the carnival business is beyond me, but that is exactly what we decided to do.

We cashed in our IRAs and purchased computer equipment to make, "I Love My Grandma and Grandpa" t-shirts, coffee mugs, key chains, etc. My husband built a carnival trailer to pull across country. We named the business the *Photo Wizard*. Hmmmmm, not exactly a Christian-based company name. But I guess our intentions were good, as we planned to cross the country and go to Michigan, and take care of my husband's ailing parents in between carnie shows. It sounded good, kind of like running away from all of our problems, and we had a lot of them. As we got closer to leaving to begin our tour, I had to go out to the back of our property to pack our old motor home with more essentials and I had a strong prompting to bring along my Bible. Wow, that was new.

Walking towards the motor home, I began to reflect that I would finally have a little time to read the Bible. It seemed like my life had literally whizzed by so fast, that I never took the time to read it, and it made me sad. I walked across our property reflecting on my adult life. As I entered the motor home and put the Bible in a place to later get to it with ease, I had a stirring in my memory. I stopped at once – some disturbing thoughts started going around in my head, tugging at my heart, and a nagging of my conscience.

"Oh, dear God, thank you for that – change my heart, oh Lord." My thoughts were profoundly reforming in those moments. I was suddenly immersed in the memory of my counsel on abortion and I became rather ill. I had the thought that I was completely transforming on that issue. I felt tremendous regret for counseling a soul in the wrong way. I was silently speaking to Him from my heart. I stood there with the realization and understanding that my thinking had dramatically changed over the years. I put the Bible up in the cupboard and stood still. Be still and know that I am God. I felt a strong presence of God with me, as HE was working with me.

Unexpected Glory.

I then closed up the motor home and went back to the house. I would not remember it again for a month, and the next time would be HIS TIME, not mine.

Our son was married and had his own business, but struggled with very serious addiction problems. His wife, Janet, who also struggled with addictions became very close to me and our family. We were all really busy trying to earn a living, but there was no connection amongst us with The Lord, at this point. Our daughter, Kimberly, was certainly not in a good place either, but she offered to take care of the house and the dogs so we could go off and do this crazy carnival thing that the Lord allowed us to do.

Our family in the '80s: Jeff, Me, Kimberly, and Daniel

Everything was in place for me to finally, for the first time since I was a little girl, be still, to just be still: No more crazy construction business with the phones ringing all day long; the workers showing up at the crack of dawn for 15 years; scheduling with school districts, prisons, hospitals, whoever needed setup of modular offices or classrooms; or the trucks driving on and off our two-acre property loaded to the max with tools and heavy equipment.

This will be a very different lifestyle, just driving to carnivals setting up the photo booth to do business making t-shirts, hats and coffee mugs. It's 1992, and I am heading off to be a carnie. Peace at last from the world.

Psalm 139: 1, 2

Oh, Lord, you have probed
me and you know me;
you know when I sit and when I stand
You understand my thoughts from afar.

Miracle at the Truck Stop

We went to a carnival in California for a trial run at this type of new business before leaving to go across the country. At that first carnival, I remember thinking I sure hope we made the right decision to become carnies. The Greater Purpose would be revealed soon. By the end of June of 1992, we were heading to Michigan and our second stop was in Arizona for dinner and rest. We took off the next day for Texas. I cannot remember which part, it is a huge state; it seems like you drive across the desert forever in that state.

We pulled into a truck stop and had hot dogs for dinner and retired for the night. We were so excited about getting to Michigan to be with my husband's parents. They were elderly and needed the visit so desperately. Our first carnival booking was not too far from them. It was difficult to sleep with the anticipation. The next morning I went to the restroom early with a little travel bag which held all my necessities. I came out and was thinking what a gorgeous day it was, a beautiful blue Texas sky, with just a few white clouds. I was walking briskly, not thinking of anything in particular, just heading back to our motor home which was about a hundred yards away.

All of a sudden I felt a force, an unseen Hand which softly and authoritatively lifted my chin to the left and then up to the sky. I began to experience an enormous, absolutely huge Great Presence in the heavens emanating powerful waves of love right through me. This force permeated my entire being with knowledge. At the same time, The Presence began to speak to me telepathically and I dropped the bag and fell on my knees at the truck stop parking lot, in total submission to our Creator. I immediately knew who He was! All communication between The Great He and I was telepathic. His words were gently resounding in my mind, transforming every thought of mine into the intellect of our Father.

Unexpected Glory.

There was form to Him. He was not in the entire sky, but had massive form designed for my interior vision field. For example, He was not behind me in the sky. He was not in my peripheral vision ... He manifested Himself in Majesty for me, in a gigantic form, in my frontal vision. In other words, He was visible to me up high massively in the skies, but it was also interior eyes within me that sent my brain the movie screen of every second of transmitted thought of the event. He was gently correcting me in all of my thinking. It was the counsel of abortion episode. He heard my thoughts when I was packing the Bible in our motor home for the trip. God came to respond to the remorse I had begun to experience. He taught me how terrible abortion is before Him.

I was weeping. He taught me how very precious every single conception is to Him. Oh, if we only knew the greatness of motherhood and fatherhood before God. He ordains life. Every life on earth is His Will and has an eternal future with Him, the Father of all Life. Every life is part of a gigantic life puzzle of His making. If a life is taken before it is born, then that part of the puzzle will always be missing on earth. We are then missing an important contribution to humanity ordained by God. The Father's purpose is never fulfilled. His infused knowledge to me of abortion was astounding and resounding. I can still hear it today. He communicated His forgiveness to me. I understood Him to be my Father in Heaven. I was imbued with the knowledge that I would only be here a short time, and then would go to be with Him, once my purpose on earth was fulfilled.

The radiation of His love was so powerful that I was completely unaware that I was kneeling in a large public truck stop with truckers driving all around. I later wondered what that might have looked like to people driving through. All time stood still for me. I had no awareness of anything on earth, but Him. I heard no other sounds. Total silence. HE taught me as though I was a little girl, and I received all of His teachings as if I were a child.

Every Catholic teaching, with the nuns from my childhood, exploded with truth and understanding within me. I understood the immense value of the Sacraments, the Bible, and the Church. I knew He was the origin of everything. Our most brilliant ideas evaporate when standing in front of this Eternal Wisdom. I have no idea how long this went on. Maybe five minutes, but it truly seemed like an eternity. I was experiencing an Illumination of a very special kind. A mini warning, if you will. I had committed so many sins in my life. I later wondered why He only permeated my being with the one sin. I came to understand that it was the sin that truly was the most egregious to Him. The tiny being in the womb is completely helpless and dependent upon its mother for protection. I do not know why this happened to me. I never will until I am with Him again.

The encounter was so profound that my entire being was changed forever. In those moments our relationship was absolutely perfect, as though I had always known Him, and He had always known me. The ecstatic love I had for Him was indescribable. My overwhelming desire to worship Him was spontaneous in my spirit, culminating from His Presence. His Love for me extended throughout the galaxies. In addition, His Power, Grace, Eternal Knowledge, Mercy, Forgiveness, Fatherly Love, Genius, and even His Humor, washed through me. This was happening at a truck stop.

I had been working around trucks in our business for years. In our business, we sent trucks out to do setup of modular trailers and He chose that particular ambiance as a back drop for His Great Encounter with me. During this experience, the Lord infused knowledge of certain things He wanted me to do at a later date. For one, He wanted me to name the baby, and there were other things he requested as well. I accomplished all the tasks within the coming months. The Origin of Life quietly left me without any notice while I was looking up to the heavens realizing that He was gone.

I was so enraptured in His Love and HE was just gone, no farewells, no goodbyes. Father, come back to me, please don't leave me, but He wasn't there. God had left me, but He was with me. I slowly stood up in the parking lot, trying to regain my composure. I looked across the parking lot at my husband in the motor home. I was thinking my own thoughts, not His anymore. I will long for His thoughts to completely fill my soul until my last breath. The Lord's mystical gifts that would unfold throughout the coming years were incredible, and difficult for me to comprehend.

Oh, Dear Lord, now what? I cannot tell my husband, Dan. Surely he will think I have gone crazy. I began to realize, I was no longer the person I was five or ten minutes before, and yet I had to continue to appear to be Terri, the woman my husband knows. I walked slowly towards the motor home.

When I got in, Dan said, "Are you ready to boogie, honey?"

It was a favorite quip of his and I replied, 'Oh yes, I sure am!"

The drive to Michigan was spent in reflection and remembering, when Dan did not have the radio blasting country western music. I would awaken at 3 or 4 a.m. at every rest stop, and pray and read scripture from the Bible I packed. Something wonderful was moving in me and I had no one to talk to about it. I was praying and loving The Lord quietly while traveling. I was reading the Bible in the wee hours of the mornings, before Dan would awaken on the entire tour. I could not get enough of God's Word, love letters from The Great Creator, to all of us.

On one carnie tour, our station was placed directly across from 1,000 pigs. The flies were all over our t-shirts and the oink, oinks were unbelievable – all throughout the day. At this point, I was crying and begging the Lord to allow me to go home soon and try another profession! During that time, I would walk over every day to pet the pigs with my nephew, Scottie. My husband's brother brought his fourteen-year old son, our nephew, to travel with us while we were in Michigan, and we sure laughed a lot.

I shared my Great Event with my nephew, Scott, and it was very comforting to have someone with which to share as he was always such a loving and caring child to his aunt and uncle. Of course, as a kid, he really had no understanding of any of it, as it was even difficult for me to understand. I was leaving our booth sometimes just for twenty minutes to Praise the Lord with Protestant bands that were playing at the carnivals. My husband did not know what I was doing during those little disappearances. I could not stop thinking of the Lord for one minute. I prayed constantly for trust and faith that he would bring us through this.

We could not even make twenty dollars a day. It was a financial calamity, but a spiritual victory.

Our trip back home from our carnie adventure, and life would never be the same after my truck stop miracle.

Three months later we would head home to California. My life was about to become a whirlwind again. A life laced with revelations of the Holy Spirit and miracles that would change interactions with my family and friends in a remarkable way. It would be many years before I would come to understand that I was to share this momentous experience. I had become a newborn baby in the world. I became a totally willing conduit for God's possession of my soul. Many years later I came to understand that I had experienced somewhat of the near death encounter that people describe when they die, but I was fully alive. This was an Illumination, and I never wanted it to end. Forgiveness is there for all. His arms are wide open. His lap is there for all to sit on. His ear is inclined to all that speak to Him, to all that pray. He is Our Father Who Art in Heaven.

Psalm 139: 13, 14

Truly you have formed my inmost being;
you knit me in my mother's womb.
I give you thanks that I am fearfully,
wonderfully made; wonderful are your works.
My soul also you knew full well.

Sprinting to the Church

Now it was time to begin to get our trailer setting business back. We had told everyone when we left that we were done with the trailer business. I will always remember going to a pay phone, as we did not have cell phones in 1992 and I placed a collect call to a client named Edward that we had known for many years. I begged him for work when we returned. We were broke and would barely be able to make it home.

He said, "Oh, Terri, the carnie business is not working out, huh?"

I am sure he thought we had both lost our minds to try such a thing. "Well, I am sure I can scrape up something for you and Danny when you get back."

He was concerned about us and offered to give us a little work to save us from losing our home. I will never forget his kindness. The Lord would work in both our lives for many years in a way that I could never imagine. Later, I will be asked to lead Edward to God in a profound way.

Meanwhile, we headed home exhausted, never having to reside next to a thousand pigs again. Once I recuperated from the whole carnie experience, I was able to procure work in my little office for our trailer setting business through the nineties. Danny was doing modular construction and I was working in sales. We were a team trying to make money to recover. During this time, I woke up every morning before dawn and tiptoed out of the bedroom to pray. I would read the Bible and pray for my family for God's grace to touch them. When the miracle at the truck stop happened I did not have the mature mind of a Catholic, but I would become one rather rapidly.

Instantaneously, I was infused with a very great desire to go to confession during, and after, the truck stop encounter. I wanted to go make a general confession of my whole life. The Lord embedded this into my soul. My guide was the Holy Spirit. I had not been to confession in thirty-two years! The Holy Spirit took over. I went to confession and told the priest that I needed some time to confess and was thanking God there were no hourly charges. After the miracle at the truck stop, I was prompted to confess with the tongue, out loud, with great reflection, remorse and contrition. In my first general confession, Our Lord permeated my being with the sin that I had committed when I counseled on abortion years before. I had not been to confession since age twelve, and now I was 44 years old. How much sin can you pile up in thirty two years? He sent me running to confess everything.

Unexpected Glory.

I was led to the Sacrament in a very profound fashion. I was praying for my sins to be brought up in me. As I stood in the confessional line, I would ask the Holy Spirit to remind me of past sins from my entire life to present to the Lord for my soul's cleansing. My prayer was to ask with humility in order to be able to receive His graces. Ask and you shall receive. What a gift the Church has to offer us. Jesus can free us, heal us, forgive us, council us, bless us, and save us. Alleluia!

I would cry every time I went into the confessional; God was waiting to give me so much grace in this sacrament. I experienced "littleness" before God, like nothing else that I had ever experienced. I understood that I was only to concern myself with my soul's cleansing, not the priests, not my family or friends. I would stand alone before Jesus again someday and there is no pointing of fingers towards others as we stand alone.

We are totally accountable for our own thoughts, words and deeds. My experience became a journey, a pilgrimage of reparation. I kept going back to be washed and purified. He gave me a sense of sin that I could not have even imagined before this all happened. The potter was forming me, a little clay pot, into his design. It was very difficult, as no one in my family could understand me. I had an incredible love of the Church! Those around me were perplexed, I'm sure they were thinking what in the world has happened to her?

People were confused as I walked the road less traveled. My eyes and ears were opening to the scriptures. The sacraments were revealed to me in most powerful understandings. I would reflect on St. Paul preaching the need for works, giving evidence of repentance to King Agrippa in the Book of Acts, all the while risking his life day and night to serve the Lord. Certainly not a one-time experience after getting knocked off his high horse.

I felt like a fish out of water for many years, who had finally found the living waters and could not drink enough. I was overwhelmed with the love of God in the confessional. I felt washed with the Blood of the Lamb every time I went. I truly was receiving major graces and wonderful words from the priest's lips that was Jesus speaking directly to me during that sacrament. I received insights about my life from the priests that only the Lord knew. I truly was drinking from the wellspring of salvation that Christ left us through the Apostles.

During this time while I was running into the Church with great joy, many people were leaving the Church because this or that had been changed. I found myself saying, "Don't leave, I just got here. The Lord has brought me here. Do not leave the Church because of change. The church is a living organism and will change through time, but its essence, the core will never change. God never changes and will continue to work through His Apostolic Succession as always."

I would try and talk to Catholics about the wonders of Confession and they would look at me with perplexity. I knew they were thinking, "What is wrong with this woman? The priest in there is not a very nice person, not friendly or kind. Why would I confess my sins to him?" I would tell them, "I am not confessing to the priest – it is Jesus in there. I do not think of him as being a priest as I am confessing to Jesus, revealing things to my confessor that only Christ knows."

The priest is the wonderful apostolic minister of God's grace in the sacrament. The awesome graces I was receiving in the confessional were absolutely from the Lord in His absolution. Jesus empowered his Apostles and Bishops in the rivers of succession to bind and loose our sins. My mechanic cannot give me absolution. Neither can my doctor. If I told my dentist my sins, she would probably run out of the building. I was being led to all of this understanding by the Lord himself. Even the scriptures were leaping off the pages, reaching me, teaching me, at an amazing rate of speed. My comprehension rate was a gift and a mystery at the same time. I was receiving understanding of the scriptures and a holy knowledge, and I knew it. This process would continue for years to come. I was a student of the Lord and would follow His lead.

During my journey, a beautiful priest once said to me, "Do you know the only difference between Judas and Peter?" I answered, "No." Father then said, "The difference was that Judas would not accept the Lord's mercy and forgiveness, but St. Peter accepted it with great humility. Judas despaired and hung himself. St. Peter forged on in obedience. You have drunk from the wellspring of His waters of grace and mercy and accepted His forgiveness. Go in His peace.

1 Corinthians 9:24

*Do you not know that the runners
in the stadium all run in the race,
but only one wins the prize?
Run so as to win.*

FIVE

The Upper Room

I enter the doors of the Catholic Church and stand with ancient armies of Saints and Martyrs, Councils and Creeds. I enter into the Living Word of God. I enter into Heaven on Earth. I sign myself with the living waters of Baptism and thank The Great God of all of us for my Catholic Baptism. I sign myself with the Sign of the Cross † with the greatest reverence, for it is the sign of salvation. What a visual that St. Paul taught to all of us. Who needs more? I know with the greatest humility that I was called to be a Catholic throughout all of eternity.

I worship the Lord with all my relatives and friends, living and deceased throughout all time. My living Catholic relatives are with me in the one bread, one body. The deceased can participate with me in the Lord with whom they abide. This is a God of Armies! He is extreme order and discipline. The Catholic Liturgy is perfect. Everything fits like puzzle pieces into one giant form. There is an Old Testament Reading, a Responsorial Psalm, a New Testament Reading and the Gospel. They always correlate, one to the other, perfectly. They are chosen years in advance and speak to hearts like a flowing story, tailor made for each person in the pews.

These are examples of the Holy Spirit guiding His Church. In order to prepare for Mass, I usually bring a roll of toilet paper or many napkins to handle the tears that flow during Mass when God comes to each one of us. A few times the toilet paper has fallen out of my lap, and rolled ahead of me towards the front and showed the Lord's humor even during this Great Miracle on earth, the Mass. The Liturgy of the Word. The Liturgy of the Eucharist. We cannot imagine what is about to happen. Jesus meant what He said, and said what He meant. All things are passing, but His Word is forever. "For my flesh is true food and my blood is true drink."

Holy Communion. The Bread of Angels. The Miracle Host.
The Lamb of God. The Manna of the New Testament.
The Blood of the Lamb. The Living Bread.
The Eucharist: Body, Blood, Soul and Divinity.

Receiving the Lord in a state of grace with faith, gratitude and great love is a setting for miracles.

Not expected, but *Unexpected Glory.*

As I began to receive Him every week, I found myself in tears during every consecration. I felt His True Presence profoundly and was reduced to quiet sobs. My love for Him was very, very great during this time and I would be lost in ecstasy.

Time stood still. I never wanted the Mass to end I would arise before dawn and praise the Lord and read the Bible and see the Eucharist in the scriptures and cry.

1 Corinthians 11:27
Therefore, whoever eats the bread
or drinks the cup of the Lord
unworthily will have to answer
for the body and blood of the Lord.

This scripture does not say we would have to answer for a symbol of the body and blood of the Lord. I could see Him solemnly consecrating His own body and His own blood and telling the apostles that "This is my body" on Holy Thursday. I so wonder what were they thinking when He spoke in such a way. They loved Him, but had to be very perplexed at His words.

"For anyone who eats and drinks
without discerning the body,
eats and drinks judgment on himself."

The reality of the Eucharist was magnificent in my soul. I was deeply soul searching and the Holy Spirit was searching my soul. I was spending early morning hours soaking up the word of God and He was teaching me Himself. I was given a supernatural understanding of the scriptures. I came to Mass in awe and wonder in the knowing He was coming. I knew that The Father, The Son and the Holy Spirit came with Saint Michael, myriads of Guardian Angels, sitting in every pew, there are no empty spaces. I knew Saint Joseph and the Blessed Mother came with all the saints. We are "surrounded by a great cloud of witnesses."It is as though the entire Bible came alive and I was a spectator watching all of it. It wouldn't have been any better to actually have been there, as I get all the scenes at once in my mind's eye. I would lift up my family into the cup of blessing, the precious blood, and beg the Lord to save all of us.

My understanding of the Eucharist became so profound that I wanted to tell the whole world. During the Consecration and receiving of Our Lord, I began having many mystical experiences with Him. His Love would permeate my whole being and almost collapse me. I would enter into His Body and Blood experiencing a Love unknown to me from this world. I was not aware of anyone walking back from Communion, no awareness of anything around me in the Church. I knew my blood type had become type C for Catholic.

There was much resistance and even persecution in those around me. I was beginning to suffer from the indifference and even anti-Catholic attitudes coming from every direction. These attitudes were part of my walk with Jesus and Mary. No pain, no gain, as they say. Again, there was no one sharing this with me, at least, not yet. Every Sunday I went alone to Mass. I read the Bible alone and was learning to pray alone. The Lord was waking me up almost every morning at 3 a.m. and I would pray, read scripture and still be ready for work by 5:30 a.m. to start with my husband. I had set up an image of the Sacred Heart and the Immaculate Heart with candles in an upstairs hallway and that became my chapel. I heard of a tape ministry named *Keep The Faith* and thus, in 1993 I began my schooling in the car.

I began to study the history of the Church, ordering a lot of books that the Lord was bringing to my attention. I also was in school earning a General Contractor's license to help my husband in our construction business, so therefore we converted a room in the house to be my private study. I was now able to stay up very late and read without disturbing my husband, Danny.

Wow, married for 27 years and I finally get to stay up late and read books! I was staying up late - studying for the contractor's license, then reading books like *The Faith of the Fathers*. I was burning the candle at both ends, so to speak. Candles were burning, chant tapes were playing, and I began to purchase things like a rosary. Oh, those wee hours in the morning, The Lord and The Blessed Mother were personally guiding me in the scriptures weaved into the Holy Rosary. Those are very special memories. I received many insights of the Holy Scriptures as I prayed the Rosary during the night.

These were amazing experiences for a woman who had not been around a rosary or had heard it prayed since I was eight years old in Catholic Schools. The only thing I knew about Bibles is that they sat on tables, collected dust, and sometimes looked vintage. At this point I am 44 years-old praying the Rosary with the Bible and taking one hour to pray five mysteries. The school of Jesus and Mary was happening every morning and I was moving through the classes rapidly.

My husband was coming out every morning with all the candles burning around images in the hallway, asking if the coffee was ready and looking at me like I am a stranger in the house. "Oh yes dear, it is all ready," I would respond. I truly wondered if he had thought I had lost my mind. Looking back, I'm sure that he did, but I continued to work throughout the week, go to school, cook, clean, do laundry, and do it all well, as I had been taught by my super responsible parents and those wonderful nuns.

I tried very hard not to neglect my responsibilities in any part of my life. The Lord seemingly gave me the grace to do it all! But I was definitely praying my heart out for my family. I was a Prayer Warrior for them even though the resistance was very strong. As time went by, I began to experience significant Eucharistic Miracles, but that is later in my journey. Jesus and Mary were my teachers. No one close to me was practicing the faith. I did not realize how incredible these events were because of the infused graces at the truck stop. I just thought that a lot of people were probably having these things happen to them.

My relationship with Jesus, Mary and my Guardian Angel was growing deeper. They were becoming my daily companions. At this point in my life, I was going to Mass every Sunday alone, and any day in between. I was walking in the spirit of God as I walked through the world a dramatically changed woman. I began to understand that being brought to the font of Baptism as a baby, to be baptized a Catholic, was a very great honor. I was only beginning to understand the appreciation growing in me that would eventually become eternal gratitude.

Luke 22:19, 20

Then He took the bread, said the blessing,

broke it, and gave it to them, saying,

"This IS my Body, which will be given for you;

do this in memory of me."

And likewise the cup after they had eaten, saying,

"This cup is the new covenant in my blood,

which will be shed for you."

SIX

The Pardon Prayers and the Angels

The Lord brought me to a place every morning where I would kneel down before praying the Rosary and pray the Pardon Prayer and the Angel of Peace Prayer from Fatima. These are very pleasing to Jesus and Mary. I cannot tell you exactly how I got my hands on those prayers. I had a desire to posture myself on my knees with great love and then prostrate myself face down to pray the Fatima Prayers.

I would later learn that in 1158 A.D. an eminent Portuguese soldier by the name of Dom Goncalve Henriques, rode out at the head of an army to do battle with Moorish invaders who had entered Portugal from Spain. Among the Moorish prisoners captured was the Princess Fatima, daughter of the most important Moorish official in Spain. This girl bore a powerfully important Muslim name. After she was taken into captivity, Dom Goncalve Henriques fell in love with her and they were married with the permission of the King. But she died young and the Dom gave her Muslim name, Fatima, to a little village in Portugal's Serra de Aire mountains. Fatima slept quietly for seven centuries until 1916 when the Angel of Peace came and taught the Fatima prayers to the three precious children.[1]

Sanctuary of Fatima, Fatima, Portugal

How would I ever have known that the children were told by the Angel himself to pray these prayers prostrate. I was led to do this by the Holy Spirit in the quiet of the night. I was prostrate praying the Fatima prayers while my husband slept. I was in the home school of Jesus and Mary. The Lord and His Mother were guiding me to read the scriptures that pertained to each mystery of the Rosary and I would receive lights of understanding in each mystery that made the Rosary come alive, a living Rosary. For example, when The Blessed Mother goes to the temple with Saint Joseph to offer Jesus to the Father as a baby, Simeon, who waited

---

[1] 1 http://www.holymary.info/fatimatheprincess.html

all his life for this moment says, "And you too will suffer to the marrow of your bones, so that the secret thoughts of many will be known."This was alluding to Confession. I came to understand that in the Lord's sacrifice on the cross His Church would be built, and the Sacraments would enter through the Church.

I waitressed most of my life, loved to cook, play the piano, read and dance. I found myself praying on my knees receiving ancient wisdom and was totally unaware that this is not a normal occurrence in Catholics daily lives. However, I would later find out that Jesus and Mary were visiting many people in the early 1990s. Many, many conversions were going on all over the world and I was one of the many. I now had two lives. One that was on the natural plane in order to: work a job; clean the house; do laundry; and cooking for my family; in other words, managing a household and a small business at the same time. I was also living another life that was totally supernatural with Jesus, Mary, my Guardian Angel and the saints. My spiritual life would spill over all day long into the natural realm, and those around me began to look at me very strangely.

One morning I asked the Lord for my Guardian Angel's name. I realize now that this is an area in Our Church that is not taught to us, but I did not know that at the time and asked as a child would from a parent. The answer was like a lightning bolt – Thessalonia. It was immediate and clear. Wow, Thessalonia, I love you. Can I really call you that?

Many years later I would apologize to my Guardian Angel for my messy car, and for having no place for my angel to sit with all the extra items I carry. I then heard a beautiful song in my head, Thessalonia, my guardian angel, Thessalonia, my heavenly friend, you guide me and lead me, you protect me freely, your guidance is always God Sent! And there was much more to the song and the melody that came with it. This song was gorgeous. I was later told by a wonderful musician friend of mine that it could be set to a symphony orchestra. My guardian angel would wake me up when I would ask to be awakened at 3 a.m. We've become best friends over the years.

One morning I was awakened inside of a dream by a beautiful little lady tapping on my shoulder. She had long curly blond hair and a beautiful pink chiffon type long dress. She was very little maybe 2' tall in the dream. She was saying in the most beautiful sweet voice, "Wake up, wake up." I sat up and it was 3 a.m. She was getting me up to pray the Chaplet of Divine Mercy and I remembered her clearly. A pure, feminine, holy angel. I knew she was my guardian angel.

Unexpected Glory.

I try to remember to call her Guardian Angel rather than Thessalonia. When I meet Jesus the Lord, He will tell me if it is the correct name of my Guardian Angel. I also began to pray the St. Michael the Archangel Prayer, and I absolutely love his prayer. I learned prayers rapidly, and this one I prayed all day long for my family. I loved St. Michael so much, and did not even have anyone to talk to about him. I could feel his protection around me. He became a great defender of my family. I began having many experiences with my guardian angel. I seemed to be able to discern when it was my guardian angel speaking to me because it is always a voice of gentle counsel.

One time I was pondering an investment that I was being advised as a risk. I really struggled with the idea as it could have hurt my husband and me greatly. We had so little money at the time. I tried and tried to get the loan to invest in this particular market and everyone denied me the money. Finally one day I prayed with my head laid on my table, "Oh dear Jesus, please tell me if you want me to do this. I do not know what I should do. Can you give me a word of direction?"

Instantly I heard an audible voice outside of the right ear, "Keep It Simple," but this voice was so sweet and gentle, like an old friend that loves me beyond description – I sensed it was my guardian angel. Someone that knows me extremely well. What an experience. I rose up with joy and said, "Oh thank you Lord, thank you guardian angel, I will not pursue this anymore. This happened right before the great recession of 2008. Thank, God, I heeded the heavenly counsel as that venture turned into a disaster for everyone concerned, and we were protected by angel power at work in my life!

Matthew 18:10

See that you do not despise one of these little ones,
for I say to you that their angels in heaven
always look upon the face of my heavenly Father.

SEVEN

The Rising Catholics

I was working many hours a day in late 1992, trying to rebuild our little construction company. Some days I would sit in our little office, 12 hours a day, reaching out to school districts and former contacts all over Southern California in an effort to get work. We had fallen way behind on our house payments, when we ran off to become carnies, so we needed to get back to our construction income.

In those days, I had an insurance agent for all the business needs, and my contact in the office was a secretary named Robin. We used to talk occasionally, primarily about insurance and business matters, when I decided to share with her about a major surgery I had in 1988, and how I was struggling with Candida which was a side effect of long-term antibiotic therapy. I tried everything to address this problem, as it was systemic. She kept encouraging me to call a couple named Ron and Judy. They were long-time clients of Robin's firm. She assured me that these people were really familiar with Candida. She said very encouraging things about this couple. The husband, Ron, was a plumber and as a client of Robin's, she was occasionally on the phone with him and he would share about his personal life even his Candida problem and his holistic approach. She was very, very fond of him. Well, I certainly was not going to call a plumber about my Candida problem - that was not going to happen.

Meanwhile, I had been praying, since returning from my carnie travels, for the Lord to please send me Catholic friends. I had not one soul with which to share my incredible return to my baptized faith. I began to think it was my destiny to be alone with all of these marvelous things happening to me. I did not know one person who was practicing the Catholic Faith, and yet, He sent me directly into the arms of Mother Church- alone.

I found myself becoming extremely contemplative, and I would go into deep prayer before I would go to confession or Mass. I had a very mystical relationship with the Blessed Trinity with my interior eyes on the Lord. Therefore, with my interior life blooming, I did not have the opportunity to meet new Catholic friends - but God knows what we need, when we need it. Robin kept on encouraging me to call her client, Ron; she was very persistent. The Holy Spirit kept nudging me as well, but I was too timid and embarrassed to introduce myself and discuss something as personal as Candida with a male stranger that was a plumber. I prayed and asked the Lord if He wanted me to do this, and it was a resounding, "Yes."

As the weeks went by, I began to build the holy courage to pick up the phone and call Ron the plumber. I had great trepidation making the call, but all my fears were quickly put to rest after the introductions. Ron was so natural at putting me at ease during the conversation. The Holy Spirit was in the thick of the whole thing. Ron was so sweet and engaging that within ten minutes I felt like I had known him for years. Ten minutes grew into an hour, and by the time I hung up with Ron, I was filled with the joy that only comes from the Lord himself.

Not only did this man know all the natural holistic approaches to address my yeast (Candida) problem, but he knew the Lord like no person I had ever known. He spoke of Jesus and Mary with so much love, tenderness and knowledge that I melted. He spoke with authority and I could sense he was truly a man of God. I had never had a man lead me into prayer on the phone or anywhere else for that matter, except at Church. This man prayed with me, shared with me, and was the instrument the Lord was going to use to truly bring me into fellowship with other Catholics - and only the Lord could have ever arranged an encounter like this - through a yeast connection.

Unexpected Glory.

His beautiful wife, Judy, had grown used to sharing her husband's time as a faith teacher. Judy was also very yielding to the Holy Spirit. Ron would spend long hours on the phone with people, sharing the Catholic faith, our Lord and scriptural discussion in prayer groups, retreats, and they freely gave of their time to the Church in any way they could. Now they were called to give me all the time in the world.

Ron would call me at 5 a.m. and say, "Sister Faustina has something to say to you."

He would proceed to read to me from *Sister Faustina's Diary, Divine Mercy in My Soul.* I was not only fellowshipping with Ron on a regular basis, but he rapidly introduced me to many saints. He taught me deep insights about prayer, and truly became my mentor in the Faith. The Lord sent me a teacher, a preacher and a leader.

I had never heard the words – retreat, novena, gifts of the Holy Spirit – in my adult life. Judy, loved participating in all of it, as she too would speak to me on the phone in great length; she loved the way I journeyed back to the Church – running, sprinting – arms open wide. I needed a devout Catholic woman as an example. As a convert, Judy is a great witness to the faith for me. God had it all planned to His perfection – everything I would need for Catholic discipleship in one couple that was living out the faith.

In 1994, we were all at a retreat with the beloved Father John Hampsch, when a dear friend of Ron and Judy's, named Esperanza (known to her friends as Essie), coined us the "Rising Catholics," after she learned about our original yeast connection. The unleavened bread was rising rapidly. I was now in a school with the perfect couple for the job. Later, they would lead me to hundreds of other Catholics at retreats. I was beginning a new journey in the faith.

Father Hampsch and me
"Healing of the Memories Retreat"

The Lord was answering my prayer in abundance. "Lord Jesus, please send me a Catholic friend, as I do not have one soul with which to share," – that was my prayer in the office years before. I would never be alone again. Ron and Judy have been very present in my life for the long haul. They have prayed their hearts out for my husband, children and grandchildren in hundreds of different situations. Their rosaries, chaplets, and Masses offered for my family feel as numerous as the stars. I thank God everyday for his gift of my spiritual Auntie Judy and Uncle Ron. My insurance company, who provided me with liability coverage and construction bonds for our business, created a lifetime bond of connecting two clients – a bond of love that will last eternally, and the dividends are out of this world!

The Rising Catholics – Ron and Judy

Romans 10:15

And how can people preach unless they are sent?
As it is written, "How beautiful are the feet
of those who bring {the} good news!"

EIGHT

Santa Maria Beckons

The Blessing of the friendship God had given me with Ron and Judy Miller began to come to fruition. As time went on, I learned about events in California from Ron. He was so very fond of the Cross of Peace in Santa Maria, and all that he and Judy had experienced at that holy site. Every March there was a retreat at the Cross of Peace event, run by a couple, Charlie and Carole Nole. Carol was the seer of Santa Maria and her mission was to get an actual cross built there in the future.

The main charism of this organization, was to pray for aborted babies year round, and to erect a gigantic cross on a hill overlooking the Santa Maria valley. They would have weekend retreats with white crosses by the hundreds representing the aborted babies. People would attend from all over the United States and pray over the crosses and many miracles occurred. Ron and Judy continued to invite me to events such as these throughout the years.

My daughter Kimberly was steeped into New Age and psychedelic drugs. I was spending much of my time praying for her. The Lord Jesus and Our Blessed Mother had brought me to a place of intercessory prayer for my children, without a critical eye of judgment upon them. I had become a Prayer Warrior of Love. My beloved daughter was off on a treacherous journey that she thought was the "Path of Peace."She was seeking a spiritual path, and had detoured into a white occultism that was adverse to organized religion, commandments, and hierarchical authority. She was intrigued by eastern religions, Wicca, reincarnation and mystical experiences.

Kimberly did not feel she had truly experienced God growing up in the Catholic Church, albeit, Catholic Lite. She had no idea of the treasure that was waiting for her in the Church. Her idealism, love for creation, and open heart made her susceptible to a theology that taught world peace, and offered a mystical spirituality.

She was young and very, very impressionable. The daughter I had raised had become a daughter of another family, a community within the Rainbow Gatherings and Grateful Dead Shows. The darkness had surrounded her and she thought she was a woman of light. I was broken hearted. It came on quickly without a lot of warning. She had moved to Los Angeles at 18 years of age, so I was not able to closely observe the changes. I knew she was dabbling in drugs, but had no idea of the dark influences of New Age in her life. What I did know was the insights I was receiving from the Holy Spirit and they were very clear. Pray, pray, and pray more.

As Ron continued to press on me to make a pilgrimage to Santa Maria, I began to feel Our Lady beckoning for me to go, and take Kimberly. The Holy Spirit opened Kimberly's heart to go with me – that in of itself was a miracle. We even took my mother to whom these Marian things were a bit peculiar. I think Mother went out of curiosity.

We met Ron and Judy up there and began to embark on a journey of glorious events. Father Rene Laurentin wrote a book that year titled, *The Way of the Cross in Santa Maria*. There were many conversions taking place, including the call into the priesthood. I was like a little girl in awe of everything in around me – the power of prayer in the auditorium, out on the lawn, small groups huddled everywhere sharing the Lord and His Mother, the fantastic faith exploding with long lines for confession and the glory of the Mass. The bookstore was Heaven sent. Many of these speakers would later go into very famous ministries.

When Ron and Judy walked into the auditorium to meet us for the first time, they took one look at Kimberly with her dreadlocks and beads, accumulated from every Grateful Dead concert; her glassy-eyed look, her wild clothes, her big smile, and Ron told Judy, "Oh Lord, what in the world have we gotten ourselves into!" After a few hours in the auditorium, they prayed over Kimberly, and the Holy Spirit came in a powerful way, and blessed us all!

It was touch-and-go the first day, for sure. Kimberly went missing for a couple hours, and I prayed in tears, until she returned. There was a spiritual battle going on for her soul and this would be the beginning of the war. We settled in and the retreat began to soften her a little. Beloved Ron and Judy did what they always do with lost sheep - embraced her, prayed for her and took her on as one of their own. She began to hang out with us, and pick up little books at tables. She would look at them, and make friends with certain vendors, and she even joined in for the Holy Rosary as the weekend blossomed.

Kimberly was always crazy about children and before she entered into the New Age Darkness, she was an absolutely wonderful girl, kind, caring and gentle. The mission of praying for the aborted babies in Santa Maria really touched her heart, in spite of the drugs and twisted thinking. She began to thoroughly enjoy the gorgeous paintings that had been brought in, the awesome statues, Infant Jesus in Our Lady's arms, Our Lady of Guadalupe image, and hundreds of religious books and art. Kimberly has always been a fantastic artist. Her baptized soul was aching for her faith, and she was moving a tiny bit in that direction.

This was the very beginning of the journey back to the faith for her. My mother was a bit bothered by all the Marian gift items in the bookstore, as it was a Marian feast day and they were there in abundance. They seemed to be overwhelming to her even though she had been in the Catholic world for years with my

Spanish father. She was rather cool on the trip - I had battles on all fronts. Ron and Judy were the most wonderful guides up there, and our sharing of that retreat would bond us together forever.

At one point, Kimberly and I got in a line to speak to Carol Nole, the seer, personally. Kimberly was behind me, and Carol would not have known that we knew each other - or anything else about us. We were total strangers to her.

When I greeted her she beckoned me to lean down and she whispered in my ear, "Do not worry, everything is going to be alright with your daughter."

Wow, what a prophecy! I was full of joy.

The last day of this memorable retreat, Kimberly and I went back into the book store to be blessed some more by all of it. We saw a line over by some paintings, statues, and such. So I took Kimberly to the line. I asked the lady next to me what exactly was the man doing up on the little stage with the people. He would place their fingers in the side wound of a very large crucifix. She told me that the crucifix was very special - The Tihaljina Cross from Yugoslavia, and the man was a deaf mute who was communicating in some way with the people in the line. As we moved up for our turn, I remember I felt as though I was really going up to Jesus on the Cross at Calvary.

I walked slowly to the step up, and the deaf mute looked into my eyes, and into my soul. He gently took my right hand and placed the fingers of that hand up into the wound on our Lord's side. As I penetrated the hole, I felt a shock of electrical love so powerful that it rippled through my whole right side! I began to reel in place and they kept coming like waves of the ocean with the power of an enormous surge. I almost died from the power of infinite love. I could not have taken anymore than what HE gave me.

Unexpected Glory.

I could never have received this amount of love in my entire body. God is perfect, so He gave me His perfect amount, the portion He desired. I experienced the love that Jesus had for all of us when He gave His Life for us on the Cross. It was the love for all of humanity that would resound through all of mankind till the end of time! I only wish I could put into words the actual experience in perfect detail, but I cannot.

As I stepped down still wobbling, and my daughter joined me when we were away from the whole scene, I asked her, "Oh my God, Kimberly, did you feel it?"

"Yes, Mom, I did."

That did it. I then thought every person in the line was experiencing the same thing. It would be years later that I would bring it up again to Kimberly.

She looked at me and said, "Oh no, Mother, I felt the love of the Holy Spirit. I felt a beautiful presence of the Lord, but certainly nothing like that! Mother, you had a profound miracle with the Cross."

Picture I took of The Magnificat Cross at the retreat

Why would He allow me the privilege of experiencing the love of His Passion? I have no words for the enormous gratefulness and love of Jesus that it brought directly to my heart. I am continuing to change through it all. Years later, I found out that a three-year-old boy had been healed of leukemia when his parents held him to the The Tihaljina Cross (known in the U.S. as the Magnificat Cross) to touch it.

There had been many different types of healings reported from all over the world that were associated with the Magnificat Cross. The Cross was brought to Santa Maria to bless and heal pilgrims at the retreat. I was later told that they did not have a deaf mute assisting people at the retreat with the Cross. No one, outside of my small group, saw him, or knew anything about such a person including the Board of Directors. Oh, the mysteries of God!

Jude 1:25

To the one who is able to keep you

from stumbling and to present you

unblemished and exultant,

in the presence of his glory,

to the only God, our savior,

through Jesus Christ our Lord be glory,

majesty, power, and authority

from ages past, now,

and for ages to come. Amen.

All that Glitters is Gold

My daughter, Kimberly, had left Los Angeles, California to follow the Grateful Dead in her Volkswagen van that she had named Orange Sunshine, aka The Slow Train. There was a lot that was going on in Kimberly's life that I was unaware of, but most importantly she met a young man, named Antobi, and they had fallen madly in love.

She came home to visit her family for Christmas 1993, and it was the great introduction to her new beau from another planet. My husband has always loved Star Trek movies – we just didn't know we were going to have an alien in *our* family. The two of them together were real characters.

When my daughter walked in, I hugged her lovingly, stroking her hair I said, "Oh, honey, would you like me to help you brush your hair?"

Kimberly replied, "No, mom, I like it that way."

I grew up a bit sheltered in Los Angeles, California, and had never seen dreadlocks spun out in such a wild way. Kind of like a hair tornado. I had also never heard the word "Rastafarian," before Kimberly introduced it that very same day. I was not aware that there was a huge culture of people that wore dreadlocks, but Kimberly always liked to be unique, and her dreadlocks were like no other. I was raised in the day of the "beehive" hairdo, sprayed with a gallon of AquaNet hairspray – who's to say which doo is more unusual.

Kim's Cultural Dreadlocks circa 1994 Teresa's Classic Beehive circa 1962

The boyfriend introduced himself as Antobi. He seemed to know only one word, "W-o-o-o-w," that he spoke slowly and like someone from Haight-Ashbury in the '60s.

Kimberly's new nickname was Sparkle. So I introduced myself to him as Sparkie, so that I would fit right in with some of their new friends: Dolphin; Frog; Lady Sunshine; and, Tree. At this point, I felt like I was going *out of my tree*, for sure. My house was open to all of these characters for visits, meals, showers, and laundry– whatever they needed. I was praying for Kimberly all the time and I wanted her to feel at home in *our* home so that I could be close to her. Kimberly told me that the Bible stated, "They came dreaded near and far," to which I replied, "I do not believe that the Bible means dreadlocks, Kimberly."

Thus, began my life with twenty-year-old hippies on drugs creating their own unique religion and lifestyle, and I was on my knees constantly. We made Antobi sleep in the game room downstairs. We began to see a real sweetness in him, even though he told me he was an alien from another planet. I told him he did not have to convince me – I believed him! His given name was Robert, and he was the son of a Methodist Minister. Robert was receiving and interpreting channeled messages, and believed that he was sent here from the open star cluster, Pleiades, to help save the world, and usher in the New Age of Peace and Enlightenment.

I was very worried about my daughter's new lifestyle. Kimberly was crazy about Robert with his long blond hair down to his waist, his gorgeous blue eyes, and his bellbottoms, but he was not my *principle* concern. Kimberly believed that she was a reincarnated tree fairy! I think it might have had something to do with the psychedelic mushrooms! They both truly acted like they were from another planet. They were smoking so much pot and whatever else that it was difficult to dialogue with them, but I never gave up.

One night while I was washing dishes "Antobi" was helping by drying them. He started a conversation, "Terri, I think I was sent here to get to know the man Jesus Christ."

I thought I would drop the dish right back into the suds, but instead said, "Yes, I am sure you were, Robert."

I had been trying to gently touch on the name of Jesus ever since he arrived, and it seemed that the Lord was right there with me, so I never worried, and just carried on according to His lead. On Christmas Eve, I asked Kimberly to go to Mass with me, which she joyfully agreed to do. I thought I was going to fall through the floor since she had not been to Church in years. She told Antobi that he could just hang out at the house rather than go, unless he wanted to participate.

He exclaimed, "I would love to go!"

My daughter's Baptismal Seal was quietly working in her spirit, and she was pleased that her planetary soul mate would consider attending! To top it off, during the Mass, to our great surprise, Antobi sang every hymnal song at the top of his lungs. These were the songs that he grew up with in the Methodist Church. He also sang in the California Boys' Choir, and has a beautiful voice. I was in total shock! The following summer, Kimberly and Robert got married at the Rainbow Gathering in The Grand Teton National Forest in Wyoming, July of 1994, and they invited us. We had always been very loving and accepting of the two of them, but this is where I had to draw the line and tell them that her father and I could not attend.

The Rosary was my great comfort and hope I was very aware of The Blessed Mother's Presence with me, and continually received lights and direction from The Lord and His Mother.

Eventually the Lord led me to a movie about Betania, Venezuela, "*The Bridge to Heaven.*" The events in Betania were so miraculous, beckoning pilgrims to come and share in the miracles and life of Maria Esperanza. I was compelled to make a pilgrimage there. The movie on Betania was very anointed, and the call to go within me was very strong. My daughter-in-law, Janet, who was married to my son Jeff at the time, felt the same calling to go as well. So she booked a ticket for me, herself and her husband – my son, Jeff. However, Jeff conveniently disappeared, right before the trip, as he was on drugs. So we took Kimberly, who truly was the chosen one for this pilgrimage.

We planned our trip with Peace Center Tours in Illinois. Our tour director, Lois Malik[2], made all the arrangements and successfully got the ticket changed from Jeff to Kimberly – approved at the last minute. The initial trip dates were planned for 10/7, the Feast of the Holy Rosary. Peace Center Tours had made a date change for that planned pilgrimage because they found out that Maria Esperanza was going to be in the U.S. during the week of the Holy Rosary (10/7/94), so they moved the planned pilgrimage to the next week when Maria would be back in Betania, but somehow this information never connected with us.

By the time we found out, Janet's child care arrangements were set in stone and our trip date could not be changed. This meant we had to go to Betania when Maria wasn't there, but I knew the Blessed Mother was, so we forged ahead. We were not part of a pilgrimage, but the Lord and Lois Malik took care of all the details. It was amazing grace, for sure. We took off on an International flight, and my prayers were flying all over that plane. I prayed for Kimberly through every mile.

When Lois faxed us our itinerary, it showed our guide's name as Jesus. She didn't indicate accent marks in her fax. My heart leapt with joy to know that Jesus was our guide! In reality, his name was Jesús, a Hispanic name pronounced, "hey-seus." How much better could it get? An auspicious name for the man who would take us on our independent journey through Caracas, Venezuela.

The date of our flight was October 7, 1994, the Feast Day of the Holy Rosary. Jesús picked us up at the Caracas airport upon our arrival, and we began our miracle journey. Each day, Jesús drove us the hour and a half from Caracas to Betania. There was a pilgrimage from Illinois that was also at our hotel, and they had two priests saying daily Mass, and we were invited to partake in all those "Illinois graces" everyday. So we had the blessing of participating in some of the events of that pilgrimage during our Betania trip, with our own guide, Jesús.

One day, Jesús mentioned to us that he wanted to take us on a private tour up to a convent in the mountains, "El Servitudos de Jesús Christo," apart from our adopted pilgrims. So one morning, he drove us up into the hills to this incredible convent that was not on the Illinois pilgrimage tour. Upon arrival, a nun named Sister Clara, introduced herself. She spoke with Jesús who translated the conversation for us. I was able to ask questions of this very poor, humble nun who was missing teeth, and glowed with joy from the Holy Spirit. She told us that on the 13th of every month, the nuns would kneel down at 9 p.m., and pray all night for the world in union with Our Lady of Fatima at their outdoor grotto. We were hanging on to every word Sister Clara said. She told us that at midnight, in the moonlight, the Blessed Mother would come and pray with them for the world.

The Blessed Mother revealed to the nuns future events coming to the world of which the nuns could not divulge to others. Our Lady also expressed to the nuns her pleasure in their great devotion, fasting and praying throughout the night. The morning after the 13th of every month, the convent floors, grounds, and even their beds would be covered in glitter! She asked if we would like to see their display of the miracle, and we were thrilled. She took us over to the outside wall of the convent where there were a dozen or more wooden shadow boxes sitting on shelves with glass enclosures displaying the months in Spanish, Septiembre, Octubre, etc.

Each shadow box had glitter pieces glued-on standup cards honoring the glitter Our Lady left behind as a gift from her visits each month. Janet, Kimberly, Jesús and I stood there very quietly looking at this simple display trying to process it all as it looked more like an elementary school science project than a miracle from above.

I saw Kimberly intently studying the cards, and I asked her, "Kim, what are you thinking?"

"Oh, nothing," she said.

I walked away, and knew that something profound was happening to her. I saw it in her face. I didn't know that Kimberly was deeply pondering the glitter. A bit later, Kim and I each went for a walk through the convent garden and banana trees. I arrived back to the convent first, with Kimberly following shortly behind. When she was done, we gathered with Janet and Jesús and said our goodbyes to the sisters with tears and left.

The next stop would be the Church where the Host that bled on December 8, 1991 during Mass at Betania in front of thousands of people was safely displayed. People dropped to their knees in adoration and awe and many took photos. Many were healed instantly of cancer, and other illnesses, and there were hundreds of conversions that were fruits of this great Eucharistic miracle. The medical institute examined it, and it was proven that what was on the Host was human blood. The water that exuded from the Host was aromatic of roses. This miracle was a message for the world of the miraculous reality of the True Presence of Jesus Christ in the Eucharist and the hope for peace on Earth.

When we first arrived at the Church, it was midday and Janet and I stayed out in front visiting, while Kimberly went inside on her own. We began to visit with a man and his wife when people all around us started to exclaim, "The miracle of the sun! The miracle of the sun!" We looked up and were astonished and blessed with a spectacular show of purple, gold, pink, and blue gorgeous circles around the sun – spinning and throwing off laser lights onto the earth. The sun was pulsating and appeared to be a white host. It was very easy to gaze for several minutes. There were over a hundred people in front of the Church all looking up and exclaiming praises to God. Surprisingly, upon our return home, we would run into the man that we were visiting with in Betania just before the miracle of the sun, at the Southern California Medjugorje Peace Conference. God works in mysterious ways.

Once we were in the Church and after Mass, I received the gift of tears for almost one hour after kneeling before the Bleeding Host. We all had God's Peace within us. The ride back to the hotel was relatively silent with our guide, Jesús. The next morning, we packed for our journey home. As we were getting dressed that morning, Janet pulled new black leggings out of a package, and put on a long, loose blouse (after all it was the '90s so this was very stylish), and we headed to the airport.

As we were boarding a man who had a television program in New York said to Kimberly, "Oh, honey, I love your doo!"

I said, "Oh, please, don't say that! My daughter-in-law and I have offered her $500 to cut those dread locks off (decorated with beads from every Grateful Dead concert)."

He laughed and said, "I love her hair. I wish I could put her on my T.V. show!"

And I realized I loved her hair, too! I loved every little detail about her! The dreadlocks, the tattoos, everything about her. She was so beautiful to me. I stood there, awestruck, with the realization that I had journeyed to Betania hoping Kimberly would change, but I was returning with the understanding that once more God had worked a great change in me.

After we boarded the plane, and got settled, I began to meditate silently and I believed the other two were doing the same. We were sitting behind the stewards' station, in the front part of the economy cabin, so there was a wall between us and the attendants. I asked Janet and Kimberly to tell me what blessings they received from the trip. After sharing, we each picked up a book about Betania to reflect upon our trip.

After a few moments of silence, we heard Janet gasp. Janet looked at me with her gorgeous green eyes looking so serious and said, "Terri, you will think I am crazy."

Her tone of voice was so serious and I told her that I would not, "Please tell me honey. What is it?"

Janet said, with tears in her eyes, "Terri, look at my leggings, they are covered in glitter."

Janet was sitting in the window seat and I was on the aisle. I looked past Kimberly in the middle seat, and saw the glitter on Janet's pants. I got down on the floor and crawled past Kimberly's legs, over to Janet so I could take a much closer look with my glasses. Her arms looked like they had been painted with fine golden glitter and her cheeks were gorgeous with various colors of the same glitter. Her brand new leggings were completely covered in glitter. I was in shock, and then I looked at Kimberly. She, too, had glitter everywhere, on her face, arms and clothes.

As I began to cry, Kimberly said, "Oh Mother, you have it all over your face and body as well."

She then softly cried and said, "Mother, I am ready to tell you what I was thinking at the display at the convent."

She said, "I thought, Oh Mary, this glitter you are leaving behind is large chunks, which perplexes me. I think of you more as bringing Mary Dust, a fine glitter. It seems more like you."

Glory Be to God for that is what He gave us on the plane, and lots of it everywhere. Janet was pulling her backpack up from under the seat and removing her jacket and other clothing, and they too, were covered in glitter!

Kimberly looked at me with the greatest love and said, "Mama, you are so beautiful with that glitter on your face," softly sobbing.

Unexpected Glory.

As I am crawling around on the floor, looking at Janet and Kimberly, studying all of the items on them, around them, covered with glitter – here comes a male steward who gets right into the "glitter of it," and wants to know what we are doing, so we tell him everything. He was so enamored by the story that he stayed with us for over thirty minutes listening all about the Blessed Mother. Afterwards, he went and brought back several flight attendants to our area, and before we knew what was happening, they all wanted to know about it on this international flight. We had most of the flight attendants, and all the passengers around us, engrossed in the glitter miracle and God's Grace was all over everyone! It truly was the flight to Heaven!

When we arrived in New York, the crew said goodbye with a huge box of Lady Godiva chocolates for us and said we were their favorite passengers ever! We just kept praying that the glitter would still be there for my husband, Dan, and my son, Jeff to see when we got home. When we finally arrived in Ontario, California, after many hours of travel on two flights, it was all gone. We were so sad. Who would believe it? Regardless, my relationship with my daughter was changed forever. I saw her in a whole new light – "God's Glittering Light!"

Our pilgrimage to Betania, Venezuela, blessed us beyond measure in a hundred different ways. The miracle of the glitter is a known phenomenon connected to the Betania Apparition site, and most specifically, the seer Maria Esperanza. She herself had experienced this many times. Even though we never met Maria during our Betania trip, the glitter connected us across the miles.

Our Lady had reconciled my relationship with my daughter, but the amazing truth is that we had no idea that her title there was, "Our Lady of Reconciliation." Kimberly was astounded to learn that fact a long while after returning. Kimberly had gone from Fairy Dust to Mary Dust, but for Kimberly and Robert there was still a very long journey ahead.

Left to Right: My daughter, Kimberly; me;
my daughter-in-law Janet
Betania, October 1994

[2] Much praise to Lois Malik of Peace Center Tours who did back flips to assure our trip would be very blessed and it was.

Thank you, Lois!

www.peacecentertours.com

Matthew 13: 16,17

But blessed are your eyes, because they see,
and your ears, because they hear.
Amen, I say to you many prophets and
righteous people longed to see what you see
but did not see it, and to hear
what you hear but did not hear it.

The Medjugorje Knockout!

We made the pilgrimage to Betania on The Feast of the Holy Rosary, and the fruits were becoming self-evident and bold. The Blessed Mother was prompting Kimberly to pray the Rosary, and she was asking Antobi to pray it with her. The first Rosary they prayed together was in the apartment of a friend, who was involved in Hare Krishna. They were totally unaware of the New Age influences in their life, but through the power of the Holy Rosary, Our Lady was working on their hearts to bring them to her Son. There was a long way to go in their conversion, and the gift of discernment present in me was working overtime. The Lord was prompting me to move with the Holy Spirit, encouraging me to constantly pray for them, *and* with them.

In 1993, long before we ever started our journey together, Kimberly and Robert (aka Antobi) had very deep connections to the world of New Age. Robert was involved in an organization by the name of ET 101*. This organization believes that people are

---

* In the early '90s, there was no World Wide Web. Since that time, this organization now has a website: www.et101.net

aliens from other planets and star clusters, and they send their members on special missions. Robert received his *ET 101* name during transcendental meditation on the top of a mountain. He became "Antobi Kumara" from that day forward. Antobi received his official laminated membership card from the *ET 101* organization, with his newly assigned name which was channeled from *the spirits* during his meditation.

The card certified that Robert was a lifetime member of their organization, which taught members that they were sent to Earth from the Pleiades open star cluster to usher in the Aquarian Age of Peace. The laminated membership card with Antobi's name on it stated that any violations of their precepts would nullify the membership. It gave a whole new meaning to the little saying, "E.T. Phone Home!" Robert being such a sweet guy would have done anything for Kimberly, so after much prompting from Kimberly, he decided to, "Give the Rosary a try." After all, Robert was so crazy about Kimberly, and as Kimberly would regularly say, "All ways are good."

Meanwhile, I invited them both to attend the Medjugorje Conference in Irvine, California, two weeks after we got back from Betania. I pretty much bribed them both using the spin of an "all expenses paid trip" to the conference. Free food, free hotel room, plus my daughter-in-law, Janet, was participating in the whole Catholic conspiracy with me just like Betania. Janet was my regular soul mate in all my adventures with Jesus and Mary. So the trip planning began.

My friends, Ron and Judy Miller (remember the rising Catholics?), booked a room in Irvine because they wanted to participate in this one, and they hoped for a front row seat in the conversion of my daughter. Kimberly, "Sparkle," brought her girlfriend named, "Dolphin," to experience another "way." Dolphin would become a lifelong, dear friend of Kimberly and Robert.

Meanwhile, I was praying my heart out, begging the Blessed Mother to help Kimberly and Robert see the "Light," of her Son, Jesus. At this point, I was following the lead of the Holy Spirit daily and listening to the still, small voice that whispers in my ear and blesses my desires for the conversion of my daughter - back to her baptized roots. I realized that Kimberly had more teaching as a child, than my son, Jeff, but it was still "Catholic Lite," at best. We needed another really big miracle to permanently convert these two hearts, and that was what I was begging the Blessed Mother to pray for on their behalf. My feet were running to get my daily tasks done, and prepared for this conference after barely getting home from Betania, Venezuela. I was not even unpacked from that trip yet, but off we went - Kimberly, Robert, Janet, Ron, Judy, Dolphin and me.

At the end of October, 1994, we went to the Medjugorje Peace Conference, at the Bren Center in Irvine, California. With great anticipation, I felt the presence of The Lord and His Mother so powerfully opening all doors for us in every aspect of the retreat. What a year at the conference. The horrific war was going on in Yugoslavia, and the adrenaline was high to send money and prayers to all of the suffering people there. Tatiana came and sang, "Let there be Peace on Earth," with a voice from Heaven. She stunned the attendees with her absolutely gorgeous voice.

There was a monk from Guadalajara, Jalisco, Mexico, who came with his assistant to pray deliverance over people at the conference. His name was Brother Peter. Janet told me about him on Saturday. Mr. Hardiman, my dear friend who was selling his book, *The Song of Three Shepherds*, in the bookstore at the conference told Janet about the monk. She kept saying, "Oh Terri, we have to somehow get Kimberly and Robert to that monk for prayer. Hmmmm, how could we ever do that? "Dearest Holy Spirit, please help us."

Well, I just kept soaking in the beautiful conference, and then after Mass on Saturday night we all stayed for the Healing Service. In those early days of the Medjugorje Peace Conference, they had various people in the center of the arena praying over people at the Healing Service right after Mass. They removed all the chairs and allowed lines to form with the various choices of healing prayer leaders. You could go to whomever you wanted by standing in their line. Janet looked down from the arena bleachers, after the Mass, and saw that Brother Peter was offering prayer, and people were lining up in the center of the arena. There were priests, healing ministers, deacons, etc. all waiting to pray over people in that area. Meanwhile, Barbara Shlemon Ryan, the Conference Mistress of Ceremonies, very beautifully directed people that were in their seats, to keep silent after Mass in order to continue worshiping the Presence of Jesus in the Eucharist.

As I was sitting in my seat, I had a magnificent miracle right after the Mass. Barbara Shlemon Ryan asked us to remain seated and reach over and touch someone's shoulder and pray over them with all of our being with the Eucharist present in each one of us. I reached out in front of me and laid my hand on a woman's shoulder. I looked at the woman and then said this prayer, "Dear God, she does not look sick." The Holy Spirit with great strength then blew me over sideways like a great wind and said interiorly to me, "It is her heart that is sick." Oh my God, I then prayed over that same woman with all my strength and was very, very anointed during the prayer.

Janet tapped me on the shoulder with the wonderful perplexed look she would get and said, "Terri, look, the monk, Peter, is down there praying over people," and she then pointed to Kimberly, who was next to me, with tears in her eyes. This was the moment we had prayed for, and when I stood up I found myself weaving on my feet with the love of the Holy Spirit. I gently embraced Kimberly and asked her to go with me for prayer. No resistance whatsoever. She got up and went with Janet and me.

We headed for Monk Peter's line and there were a lot of people in the main floor arena – at least a few hundred. In those days, several thousand people would come to the Peace

Conference. Ron and Judy were up in the stadium seats looking down. They were fervently praying for all of us, especially for Kimberly and Robert. Janet remained behind Kimberly in the Monk line. I dropped out of the line because I had a profound visit from the Holy Spirit, and I had to go off and be alone with God. The Holy Spirit was pouring a magnificent grace upon me, infusing me with His gifts.

Meanwhile, Janet felt compelled to take off her Miraculous Medal and place it around Kimberly's neck. Kimberly still has it on to this day. During that time, Kimberly had on a medicine pouch with crystals and various amulets around her neck, so the Blessed Mother was in some interesting company. Oh, and let's not forget the dreadlocks with the beads from unknown origin that she received from all the concerts. Janet said that the Monk (aka Brother Peter) and his assistant were smiling beautifully at everyone that they were praying over. Then Kimberly stepped forward, and that's when his countenance drastically changed. He looked down at the pouch around her neck, and the holy smile of Brother Peter was replaced with the intense countenance of a prayer warrior going to battle.

Unexpected Glory.

Brother Peter began rapidly firing instructions in Spanish to his assistant. The assistant then reached into his pocket and pulled out a pocket knife which he handed to Brother Peter who proceeded to cut the pouch from Kimberly's neck in a very dramatic fashion, appearing to be spiritually assaulted by her amulets and crystals. When he cutoff the various strings, the contents flew all over the arena. The Monk's assistant was rapidly praying the Rosary holding it up in the air, waving it over Kimberly. Brother Peter reached down into his robe pocket and pulled out Holy Water, and began throwing it all over Kimberly while praying intensely. At this point in time, people began moving out of various other prayer lines and were surrounding Kimberly with great prayer. Kimberly fell backwards on the floor, slain in the Holy Spirit. THE MEDJUGORJE KNOCKOUT! Kimberly was in another realm experiencing God on the floor.

When Brother Peter and his assistant were finished praying over Kimberly, they then physically pursued Robert (aka Antobi) as he had the same look as Kimberly, you know - beads from God knows where, dreadlocks, and crystals. He, too, was prayed over, slain in the spirit, and then had a dreadlock or two cut from his hair as well (Brother Peter must have felt they had spiritual attachments). While Robert was resting in the spirit, he had an incredible encounter with God. He then made a promise to convert all of the music he had previously written to now reflect the Glory to God and all future music compositions as well.

Robert was born with great musical gifts, and has become a great instrument of music for the Lord. But the Medjugorje healing service of 1994 was not over. Oh no, the Lord had more plans for that evening. Brother Peter began guiding Kimberly who was up on her feet, ready to go to Confession - it was a magnificent event for her to step into the Sacrament of

Confession directly after that spectacular deliverance. Then at the end of the evening, we all gathered together to share.

Robert, Brother Peter and his assistant

At that point, Judy began to pray over Robert and Kimberly and prophesied, "You, Robert, your name will be David. And your children will be Catholic." They were puzzled, but too exhausted to give it much thought, but unbeknownst to all of us, many children would be coming to Robert and Kimberly in their future.

We all went back to the rooms, and I praised and thanked God with tears of joy, crying myself to sleep.

II Corinthians 5:17

Therefore, whoever is in Christ is a new creation:
the old things have passed away;
behold, new things have come.

From Grateful Dead to Diaper Head

The Grateful Dead Connection had disconnected! I remember when I used to give Kimberly my credit card to go to those concerts, can you imagine? I was really bamboozled during those years. Once I was "clued in" about the drugs, and the happenings at those gatherings, I stopped doing that. Instead I got on my knees and begged the Lord to take them for His own. I told Robert and Kimberly to buckle up for the ride – they would now be traveling with Jesus and Mary, leaving the Grateful Dead in their rear view mirror. And if they thought it was exciting to follow Jerry Garcia – wait until they follow Jesus Christ, and they will be so *grateful* just to be alive!

Miracles would abound because they had now turned their lives over to Him. I was beyond the joy of the prodigal daughter and son-in-law returning. Robert and Kimberly grew in their spirituality, and began praying the Rosary with me. We traveled to retreats, studied sacred scripture well into the night, and our joy of sharing was fantastic! They could not get enough of the Lord and His Mother and were fast making new Christian friends everywhere. They were having magnificent experiences watching some of their closest friends come into the Church, such as Melissa and her daughter Summer, Richard and Kester to name a few. Those conversions required great perseverance, patience and prayer, and were miraculous to say the least. These conversions brought Kimberly and Robert great joy, especially to be Godparents to so many of them.

Richard (left) and Melissa (right, with daughter, Summer)
are two of the many Godchildren that
Kimberly and Robert have joyfully prayed for
during their journeys into the Church.

Robert and Kimberly became friends with Michael and Jenny Lou Tippet through a Catholic newsletter that Jenny Lou was publishing at home. The Tippets are also an amazing story as they belonged to a Grateful Dead Cult and converted through the Call of the Holy Spirit to the Catholic Church. They would become their lifelong friends despite the miles between them. They would share special times volunteering in the early years of the National Catholic Family Conference and would later enjoy

God parenting each other's children. Today their teenagers are very close friends.

Robert and Kimberly discovered John Michael Talbot's ministry, music and Little Portion Hermitage in Arkansas. This hermitage was a huge part of their conversion journey. They would eventually become permanently-professed, domestic members of the Brothers and Sisters of Charity. They would travel to Arkansas in the early years of their conversion, and attend national gatherings of the Brothers and Sisters of Charity, along with their babies. At this point, Robert had received a great gift for recall of scripture. Our Rosaries were replete with scripture and guidance from the Holy Spirit.

I remember going to an anointed retreat with Robert and Kimberly, before their conversion, in San Diego, California at a Catholic University. As you may recall, they were both space cadets in those early days (actually Robert was an alien). This was a weekend retreat about the image of Our Lady of Guadalupe Tilma and the Jesus, King of all Nations image. A Catholic Priest who was an expert on the Tilma taught all weekend, and the historical scientific information shared was incredible.

Kimberly and Robert were soaking it all in and were awestruck! The great Tony Melendez performed all the music that weekend and Robert thought he died and went to heaven as he watched that man playing Robert's instrument, the guitar, with his feet, so masterfully. They were being blessed, through the veil of New Age and recreational drugs.

Towards the end of the retreat, I noticed a woman praying over both of them, after the session was over, and the theater type seating had pretty much emptied out. She was in ecstatic prayer. I was mesmerized by this scene. "Who is she?" I thought to myself. She had a hand on each of their heads, and was in great joy and charismatic prayer.

After about fifteen minutes, I walked up and she turned and said, "Are you related to these two?"

I replied, "Yes, Kim is my daughter."

"Oh, dear Lord! These two are going to do great things for the Lord," she exclaimed.

Her name was Debra Gala. I said, "These two are on drugs!"

She responded, "I don't care what they're on. I saw angels above their heads pouring The Living Waters upon them and the angels were full of joy. I received revelations about them. They are highly anointed!"

Unexpected Glory.

I couldn't believe my ears. I backed away in shock. I told her I bribed them to come for free food and board.

She said, "Great, keep up the good work, mom, and keep praying! The Lord hears your prayers. I saw it, they are going to be saints!"

I was taken aback by her declaration, and replied, "Saints? Those two? Saints?"

God is a God of glory and surprises. "I tell you, they are going to do great things for the Lord," were Debra's closing words and we parted.

Later Kimberly shared that at one point while Debra was very deep in prayer, her countenance and voice changed, and they knew that Christ was speaking to them through Debra. "I have much love for you to share with the world!"

Two years later, they were like magnets to all different kinds of people – from Bob Marley to Gregorian Chant! Robert could play both musical expressions wonderfully! Everyone loved Kimberly and Robert. Robert met Fr. Ike Pueblo, a La Salette Priest at St. Christopher Church in Moreno Valley, California. Fr. Ike was astonished by their story and personally offered to catechize Robert in the faith. Robert had been raised by very liberal Methodist Ministers. Father Ike and Robert studied together and prayed together and developed a very close friendship. Robert was taking Dr. Scott Hahn tapes and the like to Father Ike to listen to. We were steeped in learning everything we could about the Catholic Church and we were having a roller coaster ride through heaven's classrooms.

Robert prepared for Confirmation and the Sacrament of Marriage. The day that Kimberly and Robert married in the Catholic Church was absolutely magnificent. It was so intimate you felt like you were in God's personal living room. I knew the angels were blowing trumpets and the Saints were cheering them on. My dear friends, Ron and Judy, were there as always. My mother was there crying her eyes out. My dearest sisters, Linda and Kathy, and their extended families, as well as my husband's family from Michigan and many others attended; and the tears of joy flowed.

Thank you, dear Jesus and Mary, for the great miracle. Robert's mother and father, Margaret and Carl, both Methodist ministers, travelled from Virginia to attend the wedding. Robert's mother played piano, and sang the Ave Maria beautifully. Miracles everywhere ... and a special mention; Robert took the name David for his confirmation name, fulfilling the prophecy from Judy Miller from so long before. And Francis, for his choice of expression of faith, was drawn to the Franciscan Order.

It truly was a most beautiful wedding. Kimberly's outfit cost ten dollars total and she was gorgeous. Their rings cost ten dollars as well. She put it together Franciscan style - simple and humble. The Lord had great plans for these two, for certain. The drug use vanished and so did many of their old friends, one by one. Robert began to play music and sing at St. Christopher's at the Masses. Robert and Kimberly were settling down beautifully into a very Catholic marriage. They also were attending a church pastored by Father Louis Marx who would become a great family friend. He was teaching them the very traditional side of the Church. They were becoming Charismatic Traditionalists.

I beheld the Glory of Conversion out of drugs, occult, other gods, and great deception - out of the darkness, into the light. Robert was now composing music for the Liturgy, Kimberly was studying natural family planning and I stood back and watched in shock and awe at God's power and love. Judy, "the Rising Catholic," had also prophesized at the Medjugorje Conference, "you will raise your children Catholic," and it was about to come to fruition. Meanwhile, I was drawn by the Holy Spirit to study the history of the Church with Robert and Kimberly and we were of one mind and spirit. The Lord had brought me practicing Catholic Christians, having fellowship around the clock, and we were having so many miracles that we were hesitant to tell anyone.

Kimberly and Robert celebrate their wedding
with family in the Catholic Church

The future was about to unfold for Kimberly and Robert –
from Grateful Dead to Diaper Head!

Philippians 1:6

I am confident of this, that the one who began
a good work in you will continue to
complete it until the day of Christ Jesus.

TWELVE

Born Again in Water

In between Robert and Kimberly's Rainbow Gathering Wedding and The Catholic Wedding Feast, a baby boy was born. Kimberly and Robert named him Malachi Daniel Freedom. They named him Malachi after the last prophet in the Old Testament, Daniel after his maternal grandfather, and Freedom as a symbol of "breaking away" from their former lives. Malachi was the jewel on the "Crown of Conversion" for Kimberly and Robert. Father Ike baptized Malachi.

The baptism party was full of joy-filled family, great food and cake. All of the people who loved and prayed for Kimberly and Robert's conversion attended. My husband and I were thrilled with our first grandbaby, and Kimberly and Robert's embracing of the Sacraments brought us great joy. What a celebration – life was wonderful!

We lived in a beautiful home that my husband had designed in Riverside, California. Through the years he had landscaped our two-acre property with picturesque Koi ponds, streams and waterfalls. I had statues of Jesus and Mary on a hill, and water reeds and flowers flourished naturally. Inside our home, I had a lot of pictures of Jesus, Mary, St. Joseph and angels, and as Malachi grew into a toddler he would point to the people in the pictures, and say all of their names. Malachi loved learning words from a very young age, and he enjoyed sharing them with his grandma and everyone else. He would say Jesus, Mama Mary, doggy, cookie, angels, car and many others.

Early one morning, I was strolling outside having coffee with Kimberly, and I noticed Malachi toddling over by the Koi ponds. It was very disturbing to me because he was sixteen months old, and had started to show signs of wanting to explore our big property. I yelled out across the yard for Dan to put up the chicken wire that he had just bought in order to prevent Malachi from getting close to the ponds. Dan said he had a plan with Robert to put it up later in the day, after he returned from the Pomona Computer Fair. Kim and I discussed that the baby was just getting too active to leave the Koi pond area open. There was a big birthday party planned that day for my sister, Kathy, so we went on to prepare for our day as planned.

Janet, my daughter-in-law, because of a separation with my son due to addiction problems, was also living on our property in a private modular home very close to the Koi ponds. Janet went back to her place to get ready and I went upstairs to shower at mine. My son got a morning pass from his drug rehab to come to visit Janet that morning. He was to be released at 10:00 a.m., but miraculously, there were angels at work on the schedule, and he was able to leave by 8:00 a.m.

Jeff arrived at Janet's trailer on our property around 8:30 in the morning. Janet's 10 year-old daughter was visiting in our enclosed ping pong room with Kimberly, Robert and baby, Malachi. I was still upstairs getting ready for the birthday party when I realized the blouse I needed was in the laundry room.

Dripping wet from my shower, I put a towel around me, and headed downstairs to get my blouse. I saw Janet sitting in my office with a look of complete horror on her face! Her face was sheet white! Tears were streaming down her beautiful eyes.

She was on the phone with 911 and dropped the phone into her lap for a second and said, "Terri, Malachi drowned in the Koi pond, and he's dead!"

I am going to try to express what I felt at that moment. I said back to Janet, "What did you say?"

She repeated it to me, and went back to speaking with the 911 operator. Instantaneously, I had millions of emotions running through me as I was in complete and total emotional shock. With only a towel wrapped around me, still dripping wet from the shower, I ran upstairs.

I was trembling when I prayed aloud, while turning back and forth in circles in complete trauma, "Dear God, I want to pray, but I need to put clothes on and go downstairs, so I am pleading with you, please save my grandbaby. I beg you! Jesus, I Trust in You! I frantically dressed, ran downstairs and encountered paramedics in my family room with Kimberly and Robert, and then I saw Malachi, with his brown eyes changed to gray. He rose up from lying on the family room carpet, and I fainted.

They were giving me smelling salts when I came to, and Malachi and his mother were being loaded into the ambulance. I quickly got into the car with Robert and we followed behind them. Robert and I prayed the Rosary on the drive to the hospital. Kimberly and Robert later recounted all the details of the drowning to my husband and me. As all of the details came in, the story unfolded as follows:

Apparently, Kimberly, Robert, and baby Malachi went into the sun room to visit with Janet and Rochelle, and did not notice that the slider door which led outside was slightly ajar. Unfortunately, Malachi did and he slipped through the slider door unnoticed. Within minutes, Kimberly realized the baby was not with them. She asked, "Robert, where is the baby?" In seeing the slider open, the search began with everyone taking a different designated search path on the two-acre property. Some looked in the house, while others went running on the property calling out to Malachi. The time was approximately 11:00 a.m.

The first place Robert went was to the above ground pool out in the backyard that was fenced and gated. Then Robert ran to the big barn way in the back where there were horses. Kimberly was running through our two-story home checking every room. They were all frantically running everywhere yelling the baby's name and the time was ticking away. The very last place that Robert checked was the Koi ponds. Malachi was floating face down in the dark murky pond water with the Koi. Robert lifted him up and out of the pond. Janet said the beads of water flying off the baby's hair looked like they were falling off in slow motion.

They had all passed by that area for several minutes and never saw him. No one really knows how long Malachi was actually in the water. After sharing and putting all the puzzle pieces together, we determined that it was probably over ten minutes. My poor Robert and Kimberly. She was five months pregnant with her second baby, who would be named Josiah. Jeff heard his sister screaming outside and rushed to the scene.

He had just learned CPR in rehab that very week, and he jumped into the scene and began to administer CPR! Kimberly was standing back from the area where her baby was laying lifeless, in complete shock. The CPR was not working. Robert beckoned to Kimberly and said, "Come and pray with me," She moved across the yard as if in slow motion and settled at the feet of her beloved baby.

She said a prayer like never before from the deepest part of her being. "Jesus, please send your mightiest angels to carry my son back to me. I cannot bear this pain."

Kimberly dropped her head on his little legs and was sobbing. During all of this, a worker of ours, a biker named

Lyman, came through our back gates to get a tool he had left in our barn the day before. He did construction work for us, and just casually rode up on this particular Saturday morning thinking he would grab the tool. Instead he walked directly into the tragedy that would change his life forever!

He saw the dead baby on the lawn and witnessed the parents pleading to Heaven for help. Kimberly and Robert both had their arms up to the heavens begging the Lord to bring their baby back to them. The power of their great faith and prayers lifted Jeff up as he continued with his CPR efforts, but to no avail. Janet was sobbing.

And then an amazing miracle happened. Kimberly and Robert's desperate pleas to the Lord were joined by a silent prayer deep within Jeff's heart, and their prayers were lifted in unison to Heaven. Jeff was struggling to remember the exact CPR protocol, especially for a toddler. At this pivotal point, he quietly prayed, "God, help me."

Jeff stated that he felt a presence within him, and at that moment he was able to administer the rounds of CPR–perfectly. The answer to prayer was evident within seconds as Malachi's eyes rolled forward from the back of his head and he was staring straight ahead. They all watched in shock, as the water from his lungs shot up and out of his mouth and he began to whimper. Kimberly described the whimper like a child crying from very far away, at the other end of a tunnel.

The cry then got closer and closer until it was completely present in our world. She had never heard anything like it in her life. She actually heard Malachi come back from another realm! The biker, Lyman, witnessed the entire thing. The paramedics pulled up to the yard, and brought Malachi into the house and laid him down, and that is when I came down the stairs and fainted.

Malachi was taken to Riverside Community Hospital. The head of Pediatrics came up to us in the E.R. and said, "I hope you all know that you have had a great miracle with Malachi."

I told her, "Yes, we do."

She continued, "This baby is going to be fine, but I cannot explain it. We ran many tests and did not find any brain or physical damage of any kind. We must hold him for 24 hours under observation, but go and tell your family you have had a great miracle!"

Unexpected Glory.

We were praising God in the hospital, the parking lot, in the car, and all the way home. Father Ike sent in a prayer team to pray all night with Kimberly and Robert at the hospital. Malachi was released on Monday, and that night we were asked to speak at a retreat to give the Praise Report. Janet walked out to the car holding baby Malachi and when she got into the garage, Malachi looked up to the ceiling at the little lone light bulb hanging up there. He pointed and said ever so slowly, "JESUS," and Janet was stunned. She began to cry. Our baby was with Jesus! He was with the Light. He knew how to say light, he used to say it to me about the lamps, but he did not say light, he said Jesus. The light bulb was Jesus to Malachi! We went and gave the testimony. The prayer group listened to the whole story in rapt attention.

On Thursday, Malachi began to act sick, so they took him back to the hospital for observation in case it was related to the drowning. Weeks before, I had booked rooms for a Santa Maria weekend retreat which was for the week following the drowning. Since Malachi was stable, Janet and I decided to keep our commitment to our beloved friends, Steven and Sekoia, as prayer was the priority of the day. Of course, Kimberly, Robert and Malachi could not go with us as originally planned. We all agreed we would turn back if there were any startling changes with Malachi.

Upon arrival at the Santa Maria Retreat, we went to the bookstore, had lunch, and I then went to Adoration by myself. I said a prayer, "Dear Lord, if baby Malachi has caught the flu from being in the emergency room, please take it from him and give it to me. If his sickness is not from the drowning, please make it very clear to all of us. Please take away the terrible worry from Kim and Robert as they have been through so much, Lord, and this way they can take him home."

I left Adoration and later in the evening we all walked over to the convention hall where we were going to listen to a few speakers, however, I began to feel very ill and weak. I actually had to lie down in the chairs, it came on so fast. I tried to stay for the speakers, but couldn't.

My dear friend, Steven, had to drive me back to the hotel. I was so ill that once we got to the Best Western, Steven had to actually carry me upstairs to the room. Once we got upstairs and Steven had full impact of how sick I was he expressed his concern of me sharing a room with Sekoia. He offered up his room as he didn't want her to get the same illness in case it was contagious. He was that kind of guy - a gentleman through and through, so he took his sleeping bag and slept outside under the stars. The next morning I woke up as good as new, and then I got the phone call. Malachi had been released from hospital. He became well in a very mysterious way, and they took him home very relieved.

The Lord listened to my prayer, and gave me the flu that Malachi had contracted when he was admitted the first time for the drowning. It was over. Years later, the biker Lyman, died from melanoma cancer at 42 years of age, and his sister told me the drowning scene changed his life, and on his death bed he asked to be baptized. Lyman's sister also told me that he had stopped doing drugs not long after witnessing the drowning. God be praised. Malachi was born again in water.

Malachi, and his hero, Uncle Jeff

Malachi and Sister Briege McKenna;
and Father Raymond Skonezny, S.T.L.,S.S.L.,
Malachi and me at the Magnificat Meal

John 3:5

*Jesus answered, "Amen, amen, I say to you,
no one can enter the kingdom of God
without being born of water and spirit."*

THIRTEEN

Queen of Liberation

While at the Medjugorje Peace Conference in Irvine, California 1994, I purchased a book titled, "Medjugorje The Message." When I returned home, I sat it on my dresser awaiting the opportunity to eventually read it. Usually when I would return from these incredible weekend retreats, I would be floating on cloud nine, but then Monday mornings would come. I would be catapulted right back into work, and it would be awhile before I could even think about the things I would buy at retreats. I had no idea how significant this Marian book would be to me until my next encounter with it.

I was commissioned at the truck stop to storm Heaven for the babies and pray for the souls of my family, but I was still fighting battles of my own. I started to smoke cigarettes when I was fourteen. My father smoked, my friends smoked, cohorts at work smoked, my teachers smoked, and everyone on television smoked. Even my doctor smoked! My ballroom dancing parents had a wet bar in their family room as this was the place they would entertain their Arthur Murray friends. Smoking and social drinking were a huge part of the era in which I was raised and they were modeled for me as a young child in our home.

When my children were young, we needed a supplemental income. My husband's work in construction was seasonal. I had waitressed in family restaurants for years, but a cocktail waitress position in a high-end country club came available to me at age 27, when we desperately needed the money. I was a quick study on all the different alcoholic beverages and I could rattle off 16 member's drinks to my bartender from memory and the staff would stand and watch in awe. The bartender and I were the "dream team of cocktails."

I soon became many of the club members' favorite waitress. My parents taught us girls that no matter what we do, do it well. During this time, a friend gave my husband and I two baby Siamese kittens and we named them Brandy and Kahlúa. Can you tell where our priorities were? Believe me, I was enjoying my own share of cocktails during that time as well, that's just the way it was for our neighborhood in the '70s.

My mother never smoked, but my dad made up for it. As the years went on in our marriage, my husband and I both smoked in the early morning hours with our coffee, while reading blueprints. I began to notice a shortness of breath. Occasionally, I would pull out my bicycle and attempt riding up a slope by our house and my lungs would actually hurt. I was only 39 years old, and had already tried to quit smoking for a few years.

I continued over and over to quit smoking, but to no avail. The familiarities were too great. The coffee, the blueprints, the upsetting business phone calls, struggling to keep a little business afloat to raise our children, and even the private moments that I shared with my husband throughout the years were all *triggers* to pick up a cigarette. My husband, Dan, and I enjoyed socializing with my parents at parties, which included dancing, lots of great food, spirits *and* cigarettes. Why not, most people were smoking socially in those days.

In the mid '80s, people started to become more aware of the health risks of nicotine, and I, too, realized that I wanted to set a better example for my children as they became teenagers. So as my awareness peaked, I would attempt all kinds of techniques to cut back on my habit. I would hide from everyone in order to privately smoke, but most particularly from my children, because I didn't want them seeing me as their role model smoking when many of their friends were beginning to start the habit. However, my husband and I continued to share the habit together as it had always been a part of my marriage. Dan had no intention of ending his smoking career, and he enjoyed sharing it with me, immensely. Our morning ritual of a cup of coffee, a cigarette, just him-and-me time, was something he wasn't about to give up.

After the miracle at the truck stop in the '90s, I was trying desperately to quit. I would notice that when I would go to any retreat, I would only smoke one or two cigarettes all weekend. I was covered in so much grace during those retreats that I would rarely think of smoking. However, every time I would return home from a retreat, the craziness of my "old routine" would fire right up again and the same old habits would pop the addiction right out. After all, I smoked in the restaurant business for fifteen years with all my waitress buddies, so this daily habit was not going to go away easily.

By the late '80s, my two children were beginning their own addiction problems, and I still had a husband who loved to smoke and drink, but he didn't see either one of these vices as a problem. Everything was becoming so clear to me, Jesus was calling me to quit. At this point, I personally had a total paradigm shift in my thinking from all the miracles I had experienced, and I now wanted to eliminate cigarettes completely from my life.

Shortly after returning from the Medjugorje Peace Conference mentioned earlier, I awakened at 5:00 a.m. and prayed deeply, "Dearest Jesus, I have tried for years to quit smoking. Please, Lord, I am asking You to take cigarettes away from me with Your mercy and grace. I cannot do it alone. Please help me to stop smoking! I want to be free." Immediately following my prayer, I looked over and saw the cover of the book I had laid on the dresser just after returning home from the Medjugorje Peace Conference the week before, and on the cover was the most beautiful picture of Our Lady (*Medjugorje The Message*).

Oh, her face, was so lovely – it was *breathtaking*. I felt very drawn to get out of bed, walk over and pick up the book, just to gaze upon her. When I opened the book it landed on a page, and lo and behold, my eyes went directly to a sentence that said, "My Son does not want you to smoke." I felt a tremendous peace come over me. I answered the page in tears, *"Dear Blessed Mother, cigarettes will never pass my lips again, ever. I want to please you and your Son."*

I did not know it at the time, but they never, ever would. Fourteen to forty-four, thirty years and the addiction was gone. I prayed to Jesus, and He sent His Mother to help me. She brought the graces. As the days and weeks went by, I found that I couldn't bear to be near the smell, as they made me sick. So this caused distance between me and my husband as he carried on smoking daily.

I began to notice that when I would be offered a glass of wine I found it repugnant. I could not figure out why I did not want to have any alcohol as well. As the months went by, I realized that Our Blessed Mother had taken that desire, too. It was God's will that I no longer smoked nor drank.

I was surrounded by alcoholics and drug addicts and I was to be a pillar of strength and example of the power of God and prayer for them. The Blessed Mother - *The Queen of Liberation*-freed me and I became cigarette- and alcohol-free in seconds.

Unexpected Glory.

Jesus is The Great Liberator

He sends His Mother to say, "Do whatever He tells you," which is exactly what happened to me. I want to *Praise God's Glory* in *His Great Mercy* for all His children. He hears every word we say. When we turn to Him for help in any matter, He is attentive to our prayers. Sometimes the Lord says, "Yes," sometimes He says, "No," because it is not good for the soul, sometimes He says, "I will give it to you in the future," and sometimes He says, "I have a better plan for you."But this was instantaneous.

Gradually I was being formed more to His Will, but not significantly changing my personality, of which He takes great delight in each one of us. I was a very willing subject. During the process of writing this book, I sent an email to Weible Columns asking Mr. Wayne Weible to please tell me the page on which my life-changing sentence was written. I could not find it anywhere as I re-read many pages of *Medjugorje The Message* to find it. I did not hear back from Mr. Weible. I thought my email probably never made to him - maybe it was filtered out.

Later, I called a phone number that I found connected to Mr. Weible's website, and Sister Constance answered the phone and told me that she would have some of her nuns read the book, and they would find the sentence and call me back, but they, too, could not find it. Sister Constance wrote me an email explaining that they scoured the book and never found the sentence I was seeking. Finally, I discovered a different email address for Mr. Weible, and reached out again. This time I got a response from him. This is a quote from his email: "Hi, the miracle is that there is no such sentence in the book! Give Thanks! God Bless."

It was 5:00 a.m. and I cried for the better part of an hour after reading his reply. When I read the book 19 years before, it was also at 5:00 a.m., and that was the only sentence I saw, as my eyes went right to it. A sentence that was not in the book changed my life. The Lord put those words on the page, just for me, and only those words, as they were the only ones I saw that day. It was a personal note from The Blessed Mother to me. I have never touched a cigarette or alcoholic beverage since that beautiful morning 19 years ago. The Queen of Liberation wrapped her mantle around me and brought me the Victory I had prayed for.

I love you Blessed Mother with all my heart. Ave Maria!

Luke 1:43

And how does this happen to me that
the mother of my Lord shall come to me?

FOURTEEN

Good Friday Blindside

I had witnessed many miracles at this point, and did not realize that it was going to become a way of life. My daughter and her husband were living a totally Catholic-driven community lifestyle with great love in their daily mission. Robert, Kimberly and Malachi were now walking safely in the way of the Lord. They were meeting many young people that they were bringing into the Church because these searching souls were so profoundly impacted by their personal story. They also were asked for prayer and teachings by many Protestants who would eventually come into the Church.

I joyfully participated in answering many questions that Kimberly and Robert's new friends would have, as many had developed very negative perceptions about the Catholic Church throughout their lives. I found that through open discussion and historical writings shown to them, many would eventually come into the Church, or at least soften their positions greatly.

So I began to run off and do a lot of things by myself knowing that Kimberly and her family were in the hands of the Lord. I would go to prayer meetings, Rosary prayer circles and

Bible classes taught by great converts. I was reading books on the Faith by the dozens. I had a thirst for the history of Christendom that was insatiable. On Good Friday in 1995, I decided to walk the Stations of the Cross with a dear priest, Father Einer, and a group of people from Saint Christopher's Catholic Church in Moreno Valley, California. This was a yearly event held at the Cross on the top of Mount Rubidoux in Riverside, California.

My emotions for Jesus while walking the two-mile hike up the craggy hill to the Cross were deep with melancholy. I felt as though I had been transported to the first Good Friday walking those grueling steps behind the Savior, bewailing Him. As Father Einer read the scriptures at each station during the walk, I wept for Our Beloved Lord who gave His last breath and agonies for our Salvation.

I was deep in mediation walking the trail, when an elegant African-American woman just ahead of me, stumbled and almost fell. I ran up and caught her right arm and assisted her in regaining balance, and she turned and smiled a smile that only this woman can give. She exclaimed, "Why thank you very much! My name is Sekoiya Spencer. I am legally blind and appreciate your assistance. What is your name?"

I replied, "My name is Teresa, dear. It was my blessing to help you."

The connection was instant, soul sisters forever! We did the stations together and then exchanged phone numbers and our relationship began.

The Lord Jesus placed us together that Good Friday, two women loving and grieving for Him, as did the women that followed Jesus to Golgotha in 33 A.D.

Unexpected Glory.

In the Book of Luke, as Jesus walked with His Cross, He turned and said lamenting to the women following Him, "Do not grieve for me, but grieve for yourselves and your children!" This scripture would follow Sekoiya and me for many years as we held each other up through devastating trials that we each had with our sons. Each son would eventually go to prison and we would have each other. The Lord arranged the encounter and Sekoiya would become a great mentor to me in the Faith. She had many years of Catholicism behind her, and I followed her footsteps from then on.

I grew to deeply love her like my own sister. We would comfort one another, pray for one another and console one another. I thank God for her special charisma of encouraging me to journalize the miraculous events that were happening to me. Our many years together were fast moving and fantastic. Our prayer vigils would dovetail sometimes and we would end up praying together at the Blessed Sacrament Adoration Chapel at St. Francis de Sales Catholic Church in Riverside, California designed by Father Louis Marx. Father Marx's holy work of creating this separate 24-hour, dedicated Adoration Chapel is truly unique.

One day, Sekoiya was there praying with another woman when I entered the Blessed Sacrament. I knelt on the floor next to Sekoiya and her friend, and listened to them praying the *Jesus, King of All Nations Novena*. It sounded like music to my ears; I had never heard it before. As I prayed with them, learning the simple beauty of that novena, a vision came of incredible blue skies with a giant white cloud ring. A splendid white dove appeared and it flew very gently and slowly circling the cloud ring, and it was emanating peace to me. The Holy Spirit was delighted with our prayers in front of the Eucharistic Jesus. What a moment we shared with The True Presence of Christ.

I had become a Eucharistic Adorer at this Blessed Sacrament Chapel on Wednesdays, and Sekoiya would sometimes be there as well. On one particular day, it was just the two of us in the chapel. I crawled on my knees to Jesus in the monstrance, and as I prayed before Him, for my family and the world, I began to weep. I pulled out a roll of toilet paper from my tote bag as I was sobbing for the Lord to help us all, especially the aborted babies. His Graces were pouring out upon me. Sekoiya motioned for me to crawl over to where she was praying which was about seven feet away. When I did, I forgot the toilet paper roll and left it setting right before the Blessed Sacrament.

Later we heard the door open and someone had come in. He began to chuckle loudly, and said with a very strong Italian accent, "Is this a new kind of offering to Jesus?" It was the Pastor of the Church at the time, Father Luigi, and with just the three of us present, it was so humorous I knew even Jesus was smiling. I crawled over and got the roll of toilet paper, and silently went back to pray with my dear prayer partner. It was always an adventure with us. I felt the presence of angels, saints and babies loving us with the Lord. The Blessed Sacrament is always replete with Holy Saints and Angels.

As time went on, Sekoiya and I began to pray that our sons would be placed together into the same state prison. The Lord was in agreement and answered our prayers. In an unexplainable chain of events, this is exactly what happened. I can't explain how unlikely this scenario truly was, all I can say is that it was completely providential. Eventually I had the blessing of taking Sekoiya on a plane to Northern California to visit our sons who were now serving their time in the same prison.

What a special visit we were embarking on. We lifted each other up in prayer in every way. As we were flying up North, a very dark, thick blanket of fog surrounded our plane. The pilot announced to fasten our seat belts as we might experience some difficulties due to the very intense fog. Sekoiya and I began praying the Rosary, storming heaven pleading to Our Lady to procure a lifting of the fog. We prayed and prayed as other passengers began to voice concerns and worries. Our love and trust in Jesus and Mary was very powerful in the Rosary. We just kept begging for Our Blessed Mother to intercede for a clearing. It became a situation where the pilot actually announced we might have to land sooner for safety reasons. All of a sudden, very mysteriously, the skies became clear and gorgeous!

The passengers were exclaiming, "Oh, wow, we are so lucky!"

Oh dear, no luck about it - an answer to prayer was the reality!

After landing safely at our designation, when we passed the cockpit I heard the pilots talking about the mysterious lifting of the unusual dense fog and they were saying it was perplexing to them, the situation of the fog clearing. I leaned my head into the cabin and said, "The Lord and His Mother did it for all of us. He is Mercy. We were praying and He answered the prayers!"

They looked at us and got big smiles and nodded their heads in agreement. They knew it was unexplainable. The sun had appeared out of nowhere shining brilliantly out of that dark stifling fog and cleared it out in an instant! Sekoiya and I were off and running towards the prison like two little school girls full of joy.

After entering the admittance gates of prison, hearing there would be a waiting period, we decided to sit down on a small bench housed in an acrylic enclosure, and we began to pray a Rosary. As we sat on the bench in deep prayer, we were surprised by a woman who came in and sat down next to us. Her presence emanated a spirit of peace that permeated our area. We looked up at her, but continued to pray as she seemed to be a part of what we were doing.

Then she stood up and said, "I have been listening to you both praying, and if more people would do what you two are doing, this place would not be here." Then she turned and walked away. She did not engage in any further dialogue with us.

We finished our Rosary and both thought about this mysterious woman. Who was that we both wondered? Did we just entertain an angel? Then we remembered she wasn't carrying anything, not even a purse, and just walked off and we never saw her again. Her presence filled us with hope and love. We both decided she must have been an angel. The sad truth of the visit we had with our sons is that we could not sit at the same table with each other. At that time, the state penal system was set up to segregate prisoners by race. So even though we couldn't sit at the same table together during our visit, we had our special time independently with our sons.

Sekoiya and me in Santa Maria at a retreat

Upon returning home, I would travel to many retreats with Sekoiya and often she would be asked to sing, as she has a gorgeous voice and had sung for the Church for decades. Sekoiya was a jazz singer in her youth, and I loved for her to sing at our family gatherings as my mother loved to hear the music from the '40s. It was music that my mom and dad used to dance to. I could go on and on about the many miracles we experienced together in our travels and in prayer. Dedication in prayer with great trust is a blueprint for miracles.

My husband wanted to find land in our area close to a lake and large enough for a big barn and did not want to pay more than $40,000 for it. Now that budget was a tall order for California in the '90s since one acre was averaging $75,000 to $100,000, but Sekoiya knew how to find it! She was very close to St. Joseph and certainly made sure that I became close to him as well. St. Joseph is the CEO of properties and jobs in Heaven. After all, he provided a place to live and necessary provisions for Mary and Jesus .Sekoiya gave me her favorite statue of St. Joseph, a little old one. The minute I brought him home and into my heart the blessings began. I grew to love him very much.

Sekoiya offered to do a 40-day novena for the land on Danny's behalf. It would be her first novena ever! She would go on to do many more, but this first one gave great fruit! We had looked for two years for a property we could afford and we were about to be blessed beyond measure. Sekoiya would take a bus to Church for Daily Mass, and then take another bus later in the afternoon across town to the dedicated Blessed Sacrament Chapel mentioned earlier, quite the travels for a legally blind woman. She really put in the physical prayer effort on our behalf. She would pray the Chaplet of Divine Mercy, along with other prayers beckoning for God's mercy at the 3 o'clock hour.

I was working out of our home which enabled me to pray the chaplet with her at 3 o'clock from my location. I was also praying the novena to St. Joseph from afar with Sekoiya. We would talk on the phone and share our daily journey and Sekoiya would tell me with anguish that sometimes she was completely alone in the Blessed Sacrament. How sad is that? I could not understand why people weren't standing in long lines to get in there to be closer to the Eucharistic Jesus.

One day, towards the end of the Novena, my husband Dan came into my office and threw down a little piece of paper onto my desk. He said, "I want you to call this real estate office and ask them if they have what I want."

I noticed the realtor was in Hemet, California and asked Danny, "Why in the world would you want to go out there to the desert with lizards and cactus?" I was perplexed.

He said, "Because it might be cheaper."

So I did what he said. When I called, a man answered and when I told him what Dan wanted, he got real quiet for a moment. He then said, "You know, I have a piece of land that's being sold to pay the debts of a deceased grandfather. I think you might be interested."

I said, "Sounds good. We'll meet you on Saturday if that's alright."At the end of the conversation, I asked, "Oh, by the way, what's your name?"

He answered, "My name is Joseph."

I then knew this would be our new property, because this one was coming on the heels of a 40-day novena to our beloved St. Joseph.

We purchased the land in 1997, thanks be to God. Sekoiya and I went out there one day with our summer chairs and sat in a dirt field on the property with the five olive trees, and thanked the Lord and His Mother by saying a Rosary of gratitude. We closed with prayers of thanksgiving to St. Joseph. Later we sold our home in Riverside and moved to the four-acre dirt field. For the first eight months, we lived in our motor home, beside an outhouse, in stifling heat while my dedicated husband developed the land and set up our manufactured home so that we could begin our new life in Winchester, California.

I loved living in the quiet of the desert reading the Bible, praying and believing that the Lord has a wonderful purpose for each and every life on earth. I bought two handsome large statues of St. Joseph and placed one in the home when it was completed and one in the yard. I gave him great places of honor and love on our property. We also planted Sequoia trees for our beloved Sekoiya.

Sekoiya and I continued to pray, love, laugh, sing and run on the playground of Christ Our Lord to retreats while experiencing miracles together at Holy Mass. Sometimes the Lord would bless us mightily with His own special humor that is unique only to Him. On one occasion, we drove up North to see our boys again in prison. After visiting with our sons, we went out to get a bite to eat, and then headed off to a beautiful Church for Holy Mass. It was a Saturday Vigil Mass at St. Joseph's Catholic Church. After Mass, Sekoiya browsed around the peaceful alcoves in the Church in silent prayer and I went off to the restroom.

When I returned I walked up to the theater style seating and sat for a while looking down at the center altar area, and from that perspective I could see that Sekoiya was visiting with a woman. I proceeded to walk down and wait while Sekoiya finished her conversation. The woman had a very nice demeanor and seemed motivated by the Holy Spirit as she conversed with Sekoiya.

Sekoiya came over to me rather suddenly and very excitedly said, "Teresa! We've been invited to go to this woman's house. She wants to show us a special robed statue of Jesus, *The Black Nazarene*, that is very famous and is associated with many miracles!"

I was tired and wanted to go to our hotel room and rest. But I saw how much it meant to Sekoiya, so I went along with her.

I found myself quickly going to this lady's car with only my car keys in my pocket. I had locked up my cell phone and purse in my own car when we arrived earlier at the church for the Mass. We took off on our journey with this unknown woman at approximately 7 p.m. for what I thought was going to be a short trip. We drove and drove and then and we started to ascend on a very steep highway in the dark. I do not remember this woman's name, but was enjoying listening to her and Sekoiya chatting about the "special" Jesus we were about to see at her home.

We seemed to drive for a very long time when the woman looked over at Sekoiya and asked her how we had come up, did we fly or drive? Sekoiya told her that I had driven her up to the prison as she is legally blind and is unable to drive. This is all happening in front of me as I am sitting in the back seat of the car with those two up front.

The woman then exclaimed, "You're blind?! Well, so am I!"

I really cannot describe the fear that rippled through my soul as I felt at that moment like a hostage of the woman who was driving us on a mission. Here I was, sitting in the back seat of this strange woman's car, with two blind ladies in the front, and one was the driver, so I just started praying my heart out! I can only say that I felt bad that my husband would never know what happened to me because my identification was locked up in the car back at the church. Maybe someday a good detective could figure it out.

However, our trip was to be safely navigated by the Lord's Holy Angels as we were totally protected and arrived safely to our destination. Praise the Lord! We finally arrived at the woman's house to view the wonderful black Jesus with the long black hair carrying His cross clothed in His red and gold gown. Sekoiya was deeply moved by the whole experience as the woman was sharing many miracles connected to this wonderful doll-like image. At the end of the evening she was inspired by the Holy Spirit to give the Black Nazarene to Sekoiya.

What a treasure from our journey. Sekoiya was overwhelmed with joy and for me I was overwhelmed with joy for Sekoiya. It was truly worth the drive! Sekoiya took him home and shared him with many of her Filipino and Asian friends who were very familiar with the Black Nazarene, and were delighted that she had come back with such a gift from God. Sekoiya and I would later laugh our heads off remembering that woman driving straight up that hill saying she was blind. The Lord truly has a great sense of humor that is not of this world, and there is no such thing as a coincidence, only a God incidence.

We had a lot of miracles together, but the greatest one of all was that providential encounter on the mountain. Sekoiya and I have truly been blessed a thousand times over, by simply picking up our cross, following Jesus, and loving Him with all of our hearts. Our Precious Lord Jesus joined two women together who were very wounded. Our relationship of prayer, comfort, laughter, tears and travels, would enable us to get through the many years of waiting for our sons to come home from prison. We became Good Friday Blindside sisters forever.

Matthew 18:19-20

Again, (amen,) I say to you,
if two of you agree on earth about anything
for which they are to pray it shall be granted
to them by my heavenly Father.
For where two or three are gathered
together in my name,
there am I in the midst of them.

FIFTEEN

Saint Anthony and the Tomatoes

In December of 1994, I headed out to do a little Christmas shopping, and also intended to get some groceries at Stater Bros. I took a one hundred dollar bill and a fifty dollar bill. I drove to Stater Bros. grocery store first. It was a cold and dreary day.

As I pulled into the shopping center, there stood a woman who appeared to be in distress. She held a sign stating that her electricity had been turned off and she had children who were hungry at home. She only asked for canned goods. My heart was deeply moved. I went behind the Del Taco which was close to where the woman was standing and I parked. I was instantly aware that the Lord wanted me to help her in some way. I prayed to the Holy Spirit to guide me, "Oh, Dearest Holy Spirit, I know you want me to help her. Do you want me to give her the fifty or the one hundred?"

I heard my answer in a very gentle, whispered way, "The fifty."

I walked over to the woman and told her that the Lord told me to give her a gift. She was stunned as I handed her the fifty dollar bill. She began to cry and so did I. I held her and felt God's warming presence all over us on that cold, damp day.

She said, "I can turn my electricity back on for Christmas! How can I ever thank you?"

"The Lord moved in me to give it to you, dear lady," I told her. Oh, it was my gift, far more than hers. The blessing for her shot through me like an arrow of love!

Christmas. The Manger. The Baby Jesus. The Prince of Peace.
The Savior. The Virgin Mary. Saint Joseph.
The Star. The Magi. Love.

The miracle of Christmas was all around us in that cold, drab parking lot in that moment of sharing between strangers. The warmth of God was intense between the two of us. I finally had to leave her and go do my shopping. I was so high on His Grace that I wanted to run in and hug everyone in the grocery store.

I went back to my car, grabbed the remaining $100 bill out of my purse, carrying it in my hand, as I walked to the market still deeply connected to the Holy Spirit.

I began to shop, grabbing the typical essentials: dog food, milk, vegetables, and others. About 15 minutes into it, I pushed my shopping cart to the checkout counter and after loading my groceries I felt truly grounded back on planet earth. Shopping and money has that effect on people. When I opened my hand to pay the bill, the $100 bill was gone. Now, that I was back on a natural plain from the supernatural, I came to the realization that my husband Dan was going to be really upset with me. Oh, what have I done? I gave away a fifty and now have no money to pay for my own groceries. I'm in trouble. I went to the manager and told him I must have dropped it. He and other checkers went running through the market looking on the floor. I took off on my own and walked my previous paths.

I got to the dog food section and laid my head down on the middle shelves. I suddenly had a recollection of my beautiful Aunt Mary who spoke openly of her love for the Lord Jesus, The Blessed Mother and Saint Joseph. Every time I went to visit my aunt she would go on and on about how her friend, Saint Anthony of Padua, the wonder worker, brought her lost things. She would always tell me that Saint Anthony would bring her lost medicines, lost keys, lost glasses, and so on.

I was very perplexed by these stories because I did not understand the communion of saints. I was not raised that way, but my training that began in the truck stop in 1992 was about to take me to a new level.

I bowed my head towards the shelves with the dog food bags and began to pray, "Dear Saint Anthony, you do not know me, but my devout Aunt Mary is your good friend. She told me about you and said that you would find lost things for us if we asked. I, too, want to be your friend. Could you, please, help me St. Anthony? I have lost a one hundred dollar bill and I will be in a lot of trouble if I do not find it. Please St. Anthony, can you tell me where it is?"

A thunderbolt in my mind gave me the word, TOMATOES! I said, "The money is by the tomatoes? Okay, I will go over to the produce section, Saint Anthony, and look."

I ran over to the tomatoes in the vegetable department where I had been, and looked all over that entire area to no avail. Sad. No $100 bill. So I went back to the manager, told him how I recounted my steps, but did not find the $100 bill. He shared that his staff too had been everywhere, but could not find it. So I gave my name and phone number to the manager and left. This all happened in the second week of December 1994. I had to tell my husband about the events of my afternoon, but because he had the Christmas spirit he was very understanding about the whole thing.

By the time we celebrated the Birth of Christ, and with the busyness of the season, I had forgotten the whole incident. After ringing in the New Year, I was working at my desk and the phone rang. A woman asked, "Is this Teresa Brownlee?"

I said, "Yes it is, who's calling?"

"Well, I want to first apologize for not calling you sooner, but we have been very active with family and our church during the holidays and I just could not get to this until now." She told me her name which in hindsight, I wish I had written down. She wanted to tell me that she was calling about my $100 bill!

I said, "What did you say?"

She said, "Yes, apparently the very day you lost it we came in with our little five-year old daughter to get groceries. I told her she was too big to ride in the upper part of the cart because she had grown so tall, so she asked if she could ride in the bottom of the cart and I told her yes. We roamed around and when we got to the vegetable department I pushed her over to the tomatoes and she cried out, 'Mommy, mommy, there is money down under there on the floor.' I reached down into the sloping of the bin and much to my surprise, on the floor, tucked out of sight, was a *one hundred dollar bill* right under the tomatoes. I had to catch my breath."

I gasped, "Did you say *under the tomatoes?*"

She said, "Yes." The only reason we found it was because my little girl was riding in the bottom part of the cart at floor level."

Unexpected Glory.

We told the manager and he said it belonged to you and gave us your name and phone number. She then said, "Please accept my apologies for taking so long."

Now, I cannot express what it felt like to be St. Anthony's new earthly friend. I knew he heard that phone call and my heart was full of joy, something unexplainable to the world, a certainty that we do have great friends in Heaven. What a moment. *"Saint Anthony, I love you, thank you, thank you! I will always remember our incredible moment together in the dog food section of the grocery aisle."*

We then made arrangements to meet the family with the $100 bill at our home. I asked the mother on the phone if there was anything I could get for her little girl and she said that she didn't want her to receive money for being honest, but they did get a puppy for their daughter for Christmas, and a dog toy as a reward would be great. They were a very nice Christian family.

From the time of the grocery store event, to the day they came over, about six weeks had passed. The day they came over they explained to me that they attend Harvest Church in Riverside, California. I gave the little girl a ball for her puppy and then felt prompted to tell them the entire story. As Protestants, they were totally unfamiliar with the communion of saints teaching of the Catholic Church. I can honestly say, we were all in union in my living room that day. There was no division whatsoever. They knew it was all true and could do nothing, but tear up and smile. They loved the whole story.

It was a beautiful encounter. They said they were very thankful to be a part of such a beautiful Christmas miracle. We truly have a great cloud of witnesses in Heaven cheering us on, who are ready to assist us in the Lord. I made a phone call to Heaven and the person I called picked up and answered with a very sincere interest in me.

Saint Anthony of Padua loves us. How Blessed we are.
Glory to God in His Angels and Saints.

Hebrews 12: 1-2

Therefore, since we are surrounded by
so great a cloud of witnesses,
let us rid ourselves of every burden
and sin that clings to us,
and persevere in running the race that
lies before us while keeping our eyes fixed
on Jesus, the leader and perfecter of faith.

SIXTEEN

God's Drive-Thru Order

As you may recall from Glory Four when I had made a desperate phone call to Edward about us going broke in the carnie business, he told us to come back to California and he would give us work. Edward did have a compassionate heart.

Edward and my husband Dan had a very strong relationship all through the eighties and nineties when the aerospace industry was booming, and modular trailers were shipping all over the country. It seemed like everyone needed office space and Edward was a new salesman for a modular leasing company in those days and gave many construction projects to my husband. Edward was a brilliant salesman and Dan always made sure that the field work complemented Edward's reputation before his superiors. I handled the office and all related paperwork; scheduling, dispatch, materials, customer relations and delegated the employee work responsibilities, including payroll.

Edward loved working with us and our years together were very prosperous. Those 25 years of working with him were our most productive and prosperous work years during our marriage. We knew his wife and our friendship continued for many years.

He gave us a good boost when we got back from our carnie experience and we were up and running again in our modular construction business in no time. However, the industry took its toll on Edward and he became very short-tempered with little problems and extremely difficult to work with as the years went by.

One day, Edward called me about a problem out in the field that had absolutely nothing to do with us. I tried to reason with him, but to no avail. I could not take the cursing and quietly said, "Edward, we cannot work for you anymore."

Dead silence came across the phone line for a moment. I knew he was stunned and angry. He knew he could trust us in any situation and that was hard to find in our industry, but he said, "All right Terri."

He was trying to regain his composure as he realized he was cursing and that he had annihilated our relationship in his tirade of anger. However, I trusted in the Lord completely and knew He would bring us work from other accounts.

As time went on, I missed Edward and I prayed for him, but I could not bear hearing him yelling the Lord's name in vain and had to walk away, as that was the first and the last time. We did get new business and those accounts kept us busy and paid the bills. After a few years, I forgot about the whole incident, and I even forgot about Edward. I had so much going on with my own family and with our business I could barely keep up with it all. So, the years flew by and one fateful evening I went to Burger King to get dinner for me and Danny.

I ordered two cheeseburgers, two fries and two cokes. What a great diet, huh? As I waited at the window for the order, I stared ahead not thinking about anything in particular, as I was very tired. All of a sudden with absolutely no leading, the Lord came through my car's front window with a magnificent commanding power. He overwhelmingly filled my car and spoke with great authority, "I want you to tell Edward about Me!"

I responded with, "Lord, he will throw me out of his office." Once more the Lord left me with no goodbye, and that was the end of the encounter.

Unexpected Glory.

Once again I was given the infusion of knowledge and sensibilities to see and feel His Presence as He came to me. It was not anything like the first Great Encounter in the truck stop, very short, but very familiar to me. Almighty God had personally spoken to me once again. I knew my Father's voice, and He knew mine. I was stunned. He did not say to pray for Edward only. He commanded me to tell Edward about HIM!

I kept pondering Our Lord's words. How in the world could I ever accomplish this one? I had not seen Edward in years. I did not work for him or have any connection with him whatsoever. How would I do it? And would he listen to me? I was very, very perplexed by the time I arrived home and had lost my appetite for my drive-thru order.

I now had a mission to accomplish with no instructions on how to do it. The Lord placed His Order at the drive-thru and I had to comply. I prayed to the Holy Spirit for guidance and discernment in the whole matter and He began to lead me. First, I contacted Edward's office and was full of joy when a saleswoman that I knew answered the phone. I had worked with this woman on many jobs over the years.

She was so thrilled to hear my voice and kept saying, "I cannot wait to tell Edward, you and Dan want to work with us again!"

I hesitantly replied, "But do you think he will let us back in?"

She then said, "Oh, Terri, I think he has really missed you and Dan. Call me in two days."

I was amazed at how happy she was to hear my voice.

I called back two days later and she exclaimed, "He was thrilled to hear you want to come back and told me to start faxing jobs to you!"

I could not believe it and asked her, "Doesn't he want to see us first?"

She replied, "Are you kidding? He said to get you guys busy right away and he will see you when you finish his first two jobs I am sending over. He also said, Tell Dan and Terri we'll retire together out of this thing in a few years."

The Lord was moving ahead of me in a very strategic way, but I would be a very slow learner. Too slow unfortunately. This was in August of 2000.

We started the first job towards the end of September 2000, and I knew it would take a month to do. The second job took us way into November. The jobs he sent over were extensive and Dan had to be out in the field every day. I kept praying as to how to approach Edward, and asked Danny to go into Edward's office with me in early December to take in the billing. However, I ended up faxing the bills because we just could not make it to his office before the end of the year.

As we got closer to Christmas, I asked my husband to go to Edward's office and pay him a surprise Christmas visit and take in some Hickory Farms for him and his wife. My new dilemma was how could I discuss the Lord with Danny sitting there? Dan would have been embarrassed. My husband was certainly not out there praising the Lord with people, and here I was still dragging my feet on the drive-thru command.

The mission was still not accomplished and it was near Christmas and we were working by fax and phone only. No personal encounter with Edward yet. When the end of December came, I went to Danny and told him in tears that I had to see Edward and he agreed to go with me right after the New Year, as he wanted to get a haircut. He was working every day; he had been too tired to get a haircut.

Dan explained to me, "Edward hates long hair, Terri. I have got to get a haircut before we go into his office."

I kept thinking if I could go in with Dan the first time, then later I could go back by myself and tell Edward how much the Lord loves him and wants a relationship with him. I was getting anxious to do the Lord's will as time was ticking away.

Dan wanted to go up north and see our son in prison in early January. We were packing the old motor home for a four-day trip, and that very morning he promised to take me on a visit to see Edward when we got back. I went back into the house to get a few last minute items when I heard the phone ringing in the office. It was about 8 a.m. the first week in January 2001. I walked in and answered the phone and it was a man from Edward's office who was very close to him. He asked me if anyone was with me. I told him Danny was outside waiting for me in the motor home. He asked me to sit down. I knew something huge was coming.

He then said, "Terri, yesterday Edward was killed in a terrible car accident. He hit black ice and lost control of the car and wrapped it around a tree. They had to remove him with the jaws of life."

I said, "What? Oh, Dear God. Oh no. I waited too long."

The man on the other end of the phone did not know what I was talking about. I felt like I had been hit in the stomach with a baseball bat. I fell against the wall and slumped down to the floor. I began to cry, pray, and beg God to forgive me for moving too slow. He wanted me to be a messenger of His Love to Edward and I never completed my mission. He sent me to plead Edward's attention towards Him. It had been five months since the *Drive-Thru Order*.

I remember pondering in the early months following Edward's death why someone closer to him, someone in his own family – why were they not commissioned to bring the Lord to Edward? What about his wife, Lord? After the funeral, I realized that he probably would not have listened to her, either, so the Lord chose me to do it. There were a thousand people at his funeral and many of them told me that they had never actually met Edward. They conducted their business with him by telephone for many years. He stayed to himself in his office. He was in his middle fifties when the accident happened.

I was devastated for a long time. I went to his grave after the funeral to pray the Chaplet of Divine Mercy for Edward. I knelt at his grave and asked him to forgive me, as I did not move quickly enough to bring God's proclamation to him. I prayed for the Lord's Mercy upon his soul and I knew that I would continue to pray for Edward for the rest of my life. I learned a very painful lesson in this whole matter. When the Lord gives us a command, we cannot move slowly, for tomorrow may never come. He usually does not work alone. If we do not do it, the task may not get done.

*Beautiful memory of me sitting on
Santa's lap (Edward) at a Christmas party.*

Proverbs 3: 5,6

Trust in the Lord with all your heart
and lean not upon your own understanding.
In all your ways, acknowledge Him,
and HE shall direct your path.

SEVENTEEN

Mystery Billboard at the Circle K

In the years following the truck stop miracle, I made two pilgrimages to the Conyers, Georgia farm where many miracles were occurring at that time. My daughter-in-law, Janet and I went in both 1995 and 1998. We were like two little kids once we arrived in Conyers. It was like buying a ticket to Heaven for the weekend, you just never knew what miracles the Lord and His Mother had in store for everyone. Janet and I were very connected when we went on our pilgrimages together. This location was an anointed place in the eighties and nineties. We first heard about it in 1994 and we began to plan our initial trip.

After our first experience at the farm in 1995, Janet and I decided that we had to go to the final Fatima anniversary event October 13, 1998. We bought a trip package provided by the Conyers Group and it was very inexpensive. You got the plane, the hotel and meals for three days all for less than three hundred dollars each, so off we went.

Professor Ricardo Castanon[1] was one of the scientists that tested the Conyers visionary, Nancy Fowler, and he was there during our visit. His conversion to Catholicism grew exponentially, after conducting extensive brain-wave testing of this visionary. There were a number of scientists that tested Nancy's brain and the results deeply affected all of the doctors in that room. Jesus told Nancy to subject herself to the testing, so that he could surprise them with the results. The movie, "Why Do You Test Me?" was produced by attorney, Ron Tesoriero during his witnessing of these events.

Through the years, people came to the Conyers farm from all over the world to lead the Rosary in different languages on October 13th of every year. What an experience to hear the Rosary being said in English, Spanish, Italian, German, Portuguese, Japanese, Hebrew, and so on. We heard that there were over 100 news stations covering the event, and during the weekend we saw news helicopters filming from above. Even LIFE Magazine came to investigate the happenings at the farm on October 13 and they wrote a 5-page pictorial entitled, "The Madonna in Georgia." In it, they reported, "...one thing is clearly on display: an extraordinary faith." I keep that issue of LIFE in my cedar chest. It's a treasure of a lifetime.

I remember one miracle in particular that I will share to demonstrate the magnitude of the supernatural touchdowns on the 13th day of October. We had brought along little camping chairs that were very low to the ground; they folded up easily and we could haul them through airports in those days. We took them to the farm that incredible morning of October 13, 1998 and sat amongst approximately 120,000 people that encircled the farm.

Shortly after we arrived, a man came out onto the porch and announced, in different languages, that "The Mother is In." We knew Nancy was beginning to have her apparition, the Holy Spirit wind blew right through us and He continued around the mountain and you could hear awe-inspired sighs in a sequential effect that was like the Pentecost of our time. One hundred thousand people began to pray, sing and cry softly, as they praised God, some in tongues. What an amazing community experience with the Lord!

Keep in mind that we were in Georgia and there were tall trees peppered all around us and *not a leaf on the trees moved* as the wind of the Holy Spirit blew low to the ground, with us in beach chairs, with the "soul purpose" of announcing the visitation of the Mother of God. Nancy Fowler came out on the porch to share her experience with all of us that afternoon. This is one of the messages that, Nancy declared, came from the Virgin Mary:

"My dear children, as your heavenly Mother,

I intercede for you unceasingly before the throne of God.

[A tear came from her eye.]

I desire every soul to be united with God forever.

Love. Help each other. I say to all of you, my dear little children,

be united under God. Be bearers of His truth (she paused) **and love."**

We all recounted the experience with great joy at dinner that evening. We retired early to our room and I kept thanking God for the privilege of participating in this great glory gathering on the top of the hill that day in Conyers.

I brought along a boom box on our trip and an anointed tape by Connie Salazar, the great Catholic singer. I would bring a traveling Catholic Sanctuary in my suitcase on every pilgrimage: Holy Water; holy tapes; a boom box to play the tapes; my little chair; blessed candles; and, Holy Images. I would have loved to have seen the motel maid's faces when they came in to clean my room each day. I hope they were inspired.

I definitely had the health and strength to lug all of that around in my forties. Of course, they didn't charge for extra luggage in the '90s, as that was pre-TSA and the airports were much more lenient. They had no problem with Holy Water and Rosaries going through the scanners.

The next morning Janet and I went to Holy Mass in Conyers. There was no music available for our Mass, so I offered my boom box and my Connie Salazar tape, on which she sings, "How Beautiful," and the presiding priest was very pleased. They played that song as the priest entered the room to celebrate the Mass.

"How beautiful the hands that serve the wine and the bread and the children of the earth. How beautiful the feet that walked the long dusty road and the hill to the Cross."

Oh, how I loved hearing that gorgeous song as Father walked slowly to the altar to serve and celebrate Jesus Christ in Holy Mass. I felt so very blessed to be able to provide the music for the Mass. I was experiencing the Real Presence of Jesus Christ at the Mass in His intense love with my eyes closed when I saw a monk in a brown habit come into my left mind's eye just staring at me with love. I softly said out loud, "Priest?" I was confused. I did not know who the man was. He did not speak to me, but he stared at me for a while with a gentle look. It was during the consecration of the bread and wine.

Unexpected Glory.

When Mass ended, I stood there for a little while still wondering who came to visit me. Outside I told Janet all about it. She said, "Well, Terri, who do you think it was?"

I replied, "Janet, I do not know, but he was studying me with love and he was as clear to me as you are, but he never spoke."

From there we went over to the book store and walked in. Hanging over the inside entrance was a large picture of the man that had just come to me. I was stunned!

I went to a lady over at a desk and asked her who he was. "Why, don't you know? That is Padre Pio. He is the Patron Saint of the Conyers farm."

I tried to soak it all in as I was in shock. I did not know who Padre Pio was as I still had so much to learn.

When we got back home from Conyers, I read everything I could get my hands on about Padre Pio and in no time I knew Saint Pio! I began to pray daily *The Efficacious Novena to the Sacred Heart of Jesus* which is the novena that Padre Pio prayed for 50 years for all those who petitioned him. I loved the Sacred Heart, so it was as natural to me as the sun coming up.

It begins with:

"Oh, my Jesus, You have said:

Truly I say to you,

ask and you will receive,

seek and you will find,

knock and it will be opened to you.

Behold, Lord, I knock, I seek and I ask for the grace of (insert my petition).

Our Father...Hail Mary...Glory Be.

Sacred Heart of Jesus, I place all my trust in you."

And it goes on. I prayed this efficacious novena everyday in my morning prayers for all my loved ones and those who asked for prayers.

About a year later, I received a phone call from my sister, Kathryn. "Hi Trese, how are you?"

I replied, "Oh, I am fine sis. How are you?"

"Well, I am wondering when you put the billboard up on Van Buren Blvd. at the Circle K?"

I thought she was kidding. "The what?" I queried back to her.

"Oh come on, Trese, when did you do it?"

"Kath, I do not know what you are talking about, seriously. I could never come up with the kind of money to put up a billboard."

"Well," she continued, "you had better grab your camera, get in your car and drive up there because it looks like your handiwork."

Kathryn always had a great gift of holy insight, however, I surely did not put up a billboard. I would later be astonished that she connected me to what I was about to see. It was surely amazing grace working through her. I'll always be grateful for Kathryn's compassionate heart, following the lead of the Holy Spirit. She has been a great prayer partner uniting with me through the years to pray for my family. I'm so blessed to have such a loving, little sister. So, I jumped in the car with a camera and drove to the Circle K which is about a mile from my front door.

My Voyager van at the Circle K sitting under my daily prayer

I stood there and cried tears of joy. *"Ask and you will receive,"* with a large beautiful picture of Jesus staring down at me from the billboard. This was the scripture prayer that I was praying everyday for months since I had returned from Conyers. It was a big holy hug of a billboard seemingly direct from Jesus and my new friend Padre Pio, later to become Saint Pio.

A few months later, I walked into the Circle K and asked them if they knew who put the billboard up. They said that no one seemed to know. It was a mystery. It was up for over a year. I went back and asked again months later, but it was still a total mystery to everyone that worked in the Circle K. I would pass the billboard everyday when I would leave my house and felt a surge of grace as I drove by. I would remember the Mass in Conyers, Georgia when a very beautiful saint paid me a visit and introduced himself into my life.

The Holy Mass. The Eucharist. The Mother of God.
The Priest as the Hands and Feet that Serve.
And a Saint who had the Stigmata for over 50 years.
Saint Pio Pray for Us.

[1] Defending Faith and Science. YouTube video: the-anointed-one.com/BBU84/biblicalstupidity/science.htm

Luke 11:9

And I tell you, ask and you will receive;
seek and you will find;
knock and the door will be opened to you.

EIGHTEEN

Divine Mercy at the Jordan River

Linda Maria is my baby sister. I was nine when she was born, and our family had just begun our new lives in La Mirada after leaving Los Angeles. Since I was married at 17, Linda was only eight when I left the home for my new married life. Around that time, many financial burdens impacted our parents' lives creating a situation where our mother was called to work a second job outside the home in order to help meet their monthly bills which caused Linda to be home alone quite often or with our dad in the evenings.

Linda had such a different rearing than me, but our Catholic paternal grandmother, Asunción, made sure that the baptismal Sacrament made it to Linda's soul just after her first birthday. Within two weeks of her baptism, Asunción, passed away, but not before all three of her granddaughters received their Catholic baptismal seals.

When I was little, mom was home on the weekends and she loved to teach me to cook, and take care of our household while dad taught me how to clean like nobody's business. When Linda was growing up, our parents owned a restaurant and then moved on to a tool and die business out of the home. Their lives were all about business during her childhood. Oftentimes, our mother was working late in the home office and that was when she taught Linda many of the office skills she would use as a young woman in the business world. These were not the types of activities your typical 12-year old girl would be doing during her summer evenings. Instead, my little sister was learning how to type 100 WPM on an old manual typewriter.

I will never understand how our mother managed to embellish each daughter's specific talents while running a restaurant, then later a small tool business, while continuing to manage our household. In the evenings, when mom was working and Linda was home with dad, the two of them would often play board games or my dad would teach her his favorite card games.

Linda was a quiet child, but always very responsible and willing to help. She would come and stay with my husband and me and our little son, Jeff, during summer vacations and often on the weekends. Jeff and Linda are only nine years apart and Linda adored being with her nephew. My husband loved to camp, fish and water ski and Linda shared in many of our camping trips. Those camping years were fantastic memories with the silly games we played and all the water sports and the cookouts. My husband Dan was a great water skier and he taught Linda when she was a little girl. I water skied under the water! I had no gifts in this area.

I was the camp leader; cooking, cleaning up in the tent, mom and dad's gifts in action. We did many of these trips during her growing up years and we were all very close. Linda had a beautiful loving heart and always had a desire to help others. She loved helping with baby Jeff and hanging out with our family. When Kimberly was born in 1972, Linda had lots of sleepovers with us, having a blast playing like a big sister with both her niece and nephew. As she grew, I helped her learn to drive and she became a very independent teenager, with a job at age sixteen while maintaining high grades through high school.

During her teenage years, there was very little time spent in the Church. Our parents continued to go to Mass only occasionally once we moved to La Mirada. This was probably due to the fact that once our grandparents passed away they were no longer around to encourage mom and dad to go. I had already married, and moved out of the home at age 17, when Linda was only 8. However, I do recall the day of Linda's First Holy Communion and how she recounted to me that it was one of her most favorite days ever – "I felt like an angel!"

At 18, Linda moved out into her own apartment and shortly thereafter, she married a man that she met through our mother's work at one of her retail jobs. My mother married young; her mother married young and I married young; so the tradition continued with Linda. She married him in the Catholic Church, but neither one of them understood the true Sacrament of Marriage, none of us in the family did at the time. Her husband revealed to her very soon after they were married that he did not want to have children.

I saw Linda become more and more involved in her work. I'm sure it was a way of managing the emptiness of a fruitless marriage. Early on, I noticed that her and her husband were not practicing their faith as they were not going to Mass on Sundays, which was perplexing since they got married in the Church. It should not have been a surprise when five years later, the marriage fell apart and they divorced.

As the years flew by, I was busy with my own life, but I do remember Linda being very involved with her career and she was not practicing her Catholic faith. I'm sure it had something to do with the way she felt being divorced. I came to understand that as a divorced woman, Linda expressed that she didn't always feel a warm welcome from women in the Church.

Back in the '80s, divorced women may have felt more judged by people in the Church. A sentiment that is still present is that people who go through a divorce typically feel wounded, vulnerable, isolated and alone – whether they are men or women.

From my perspective, it would have been very difficult for Linda to forge ahead alone towards the Church, most especially since none of us knew how to counsel her on doing so.

In 1992, Linda eloped with a man she had been dating for over a year. They had a civil marriage in Santa Maria, California, and my husband and I stood up as witnesses. It was shortly before the Truck Stop Miracle. We brought our carnie trailer to the event, and actually had our first booking at the Santa Maria Fairgrounds that same weekend. We made Linda and her husband mugs, key chains, and even dolls with their wedding pictures on them. What creative wedding gifts - you can see where our priorities were!

Her husband was an agnostic and Linda was "spiritual," and she continued her busy life with work and social activities after her marriage. Her first year of marriage coincided with my great truck stop miracle, so I was very busy too - going to retreats and soaking up the Holy Spirit whenever I could. We were living very different lives at the time and saw each other mostly at birthdays and special family occasions.

Years went by, and I began to pray for all my family members like I had never prayed before and Linda was in the "Top Ten" of souls receiving my daily prayers. I saw Linda looking through my crystal-clear Catholic spectacles as living in a worldly marriage. I could see that Linda's husband was very uncomfortable praying before our meals at family gatherings, as he was not raised that way. The graces of Linda's Baptismal Seal had not yet come to fruition. I began to storm heaven for her. Every day for three consecutive years, I prayed the following private prayer during the Divine Mercy Chaplet at 3:00 p.m., the Hour of Mercy:

"Lord, Jesus, claim your daughter back by the seal of her baptism."

Linda and her husband started to have marital problems after their son, Ethan, was born in 1999. I know that Linda was so happy to finally have her beautiful baby boy, Ethan, but spiritually she began to seek comfort as the marriage was pulling apart at the seams. Linda had a Presbyterian Church in her neighborhood and eventually she took Ethan and our mother there on several occasions in 2001, but I remember Linda expressing that she didn't feel a connection to that particular Christian expression. She was on a journey and she was not yet at her destination.

When her marriage finally fell apart she was devastated. She tried very hard to put her marriage back together, but to no avail. I would tell her, "When the roots are shallow, the tree will fall."

I never felt lead by the Holy Spirit to mention the Catholic Church to Linda, I just listened to her anguish nightly on the telephone after she would put Ethan to bed, and she was all alone – physically, emotionally and spiritually. Sometimes we would talk for two to three hours at a time and I would pray for God's Will to please be done in her life. I kept praying and praying for her, as I watched her suffering and free falling into despair.

Once her husband left the home, she was passionate about having a seamless parental environment for her then three-year old son. After working through the visitation schedule with Ethan's father, she established that he would visit their son in her home every Sunday and Monday rather than Ethan going back and forth to his new bachelor apartment causing confusion and instability for my nephew. His first official visit was on Sunday, January 6, 2002. Linda left the home in an effort for her husband to feel comfortable with his son alone, as I think she was hoping to encourage this type of visitation as a pattern. What she didn't realize was she was about to embark on her own miraculous journey.

When she drove away from the house that afternoon of the first visit, she told me that she couldn't stop sobbing and said to herself in the car, "Where will I go every Sunday when Tony comes to visit our son?"

She felt like an outcast. She pulled over and called a close friend hoping she would invite her over, but was instead encouraged to see a movie as a distraction. Linda later told me that her brain couldn't absorb any entertainment – what she needed was solace. I knew in my heart what she needed was the Lord.

So she drove; and drove. She didn't even know where she was going when she turned her car into St. Cecilia's Catholic Church parking lot in Tustin, California. She sat there in the parking lot dazed, wondering why she was there. She had not been a practicing Catholic for over 25 years. She went into the Church and began to sit at the different alcoves finding herself in deep prayer and communion with the Holy Spirit – the very solace she was searching for. Linda first knelt at the St. Joseph alcove where an elderly Filipino woman was kneeling and chanting the Rosary in song, in her native language.

Linda later commented to me about it, as it was melodic and holy and brought her great peace. I knew then that the Holy Spirit had moved her. It was 3:00 p.m. when Linda entered the Church – the Hour of Divine Mercy, and at 4:45 people started entering the Church for the 5:00 p.m. Mass. Linda was surprised that people were coming to Church on Saturday late afternoon, since that's how "out-of-Catholic-touch" she was. She continued to sit at the back of the Church and listened intently to each word of the Mass. She cried. She prayed, and she began her healing.

Her first day back in the Church was on the Feast Day of the Epiphany of Our Lord, and she always said it was her personal Epiphany as well. When Linda got home from this divine appointment, she couldn't wait to call me and share her experience. She also shared it with our mother, and she told both of us that she was going to confession and Mass the following weekend. My mother leapt for joy that her daughter Linda was turning towards Jesus and the Sacraments! Our mother felt powerfully drawn to the Sacraments, as they brought her great joy through the years.

For the first time in years, my baby sister expressed that she profoundly felt God's love and comfort and she would never be the same. Linda was beginning a new journey through a very heartbreaking divorce. I watched her take one step at a time – first, an evening Mass that lifted her soul to God which was then followed by her desire to go to Confession. Our mother came over to my house the day Linda went to Confession and prayed with me (just her and I) for the first time in our lives. We held hands and felt the fire of the Holy Spirit pouring all over us, all through us and were crying tears of joy. We were so filled with the Holy Spirit I thought my mother and I would fly right through the roof.

We prayed for the priest to give Linda special words from Jesus that she would know were from Him. We prayed for great understanding and kindness from the priest to welcome her back into the Church, as it had been years since Linda had been to Confession. My mother was in total agreement with me in every prayer that afternoon. She would utter a prayer that I was thinking and vice a versa. We prayed as one for Linda for almost an hour while she was in the Church. I will never forget it. It was the closest I had ever been with my Mother in prayer.

Linda later shared with us a prayer that her priest gave her in that First Confession and we knew that our prayers for Linda had been answered:

> *"God, thank you for all that you've given me.*
> *God, thank you for all that you've taken from me.*

God, thank you for what I have left."
Father Bob's Confessional Gift to Linda

Through the years, my mother was slowly becoming more Catholic in her heart. It is a way of thinking that is not easily described. Mother truly desired Linda to experience a great Confession. On that Sunday after her Confession, she had Holy Communion on the Feast Day of the Baptism of Our Lord – her First Communion in over 25 years.

I went to my Church that same Sunday at St. Vincent Ferrer in Sun City, California, and I had no idea that I was in for the greatest miracle that day as well. Before beginning the Mass, the priest actually stepped off the altar, which was highly unusual, and said to all of us, "Do you all know what day it is today? It is the Feast of the Baptism of the Lord, and so it is the Feast of your Baptism as well! Jesus set the example of what we are to do when His cousin, John the Baptist, poured water on the Lord in the Jordan River."

I thought I would fall out of the pew!

Unexpected Glory.

The Lord wanted me to know He heard my daily prayer in the Chaplet, and He gave it His special Signature Blessing that morning. I was standing in the Waters of Grace with my little sister Linda that morning, as close to the River Jordan as we would ever come. My three-year prayer of Divine Mercy had been answered.

"Lord, Jesus, claim your daughter back by the seal of her baptism."

Linda's return to the Church was like everything else she does – with purpose and investigation. She went to many conferences, Bible studies, and read as many books as she could about the Catholic faith – and all of these experiences brought Linda fellowship. St. Cecilia was at the forefront of Linda's conversion, leading her to become involved in the California Master's Chorale with her first concert, being a Latin Mass that had never been sung in the U.S. This could only be orchestrated by our Father in heaven. My daughter, Kimberly, and I had prayed every day for Linda to have the gift of joy after her marital separation, and by Linda's conversion year's end she would participate in a Christmas concert entitled, "Journey to Joy," and she never stopped smiling.

After Linda's divorce, she came to me and asked about the process of annulment for her Catholic marriage. I walked with her through each step. I witnessed the depth of healing that comes from the annulment process, as Linda went through months of self-reflection and prayer, learning what a true Catholic marriage could have been. I watched Linda grow in her Catholic faith, as she put in the time, and the effort, in moving slowly through the various annulment stages. God mightily blessed her for it. Linda's Catholic marriage was annulled and it was a spiritual cleansing and a new beginning for my little sister. I was so full of joy to now have Linda in which to fellowship, go to

Mass; pray the Rosary; the Chaplet of Divine Mercy and share the Bible.

Her son, Ethan, was baptized in the Church a few months after Linda's conversion, and his father attended. The Holy Spirit enabled Linda to handle her separation and divorce from her husband with great love and forgiveness. I watched how she managed the situation which could only have been divinely inspired. To this day, her son's father is still involved with his son, Ethan, and Ethan has been so blessed with a mother who has guided him in the faith from the day of his baptism. He has continued on his faith journey – excelling in Catholic School and has been to many Catholic Conferences, altar serves every week, as he loves to participate actively in his faith. He prays for his father's conversion, and so we go as Catholics.

Baby sister, Linda, with our paternal grandparents,
Asunción and Pedro, on the day of her baptism.
Grandma passed away one week after Linda's baptism.

My paternal grandparents were baptized, my parents were baptized, their three daughters were baptized, all their grandchildren were baptized, and now Ethan was baptized. I prayed for your will, Lord. I did my best, and the Lord of Divine Mercy did the rest.

September 2013 Me and Linda

July 2014 Ethan serving the Feast of the Sacred Heart Mass with the Most Reverend Gerald R. Barnes

Matthew 28:19

Go, therefore, and make disciples of all nations,
baptizing them in the name of the Father,
and of the Son, and of the Holy Spirit.

NINETEEN

A Butterfly in My Life

After the truck stop miracle, I was driven to find as many Catholic bible lecture classes that I could fit into my hectic life schedule. In 1997, I enrolled in a multi-week course on Christendom presented by a master historian in the Riverside, California area. Feelings of anticipation and excitement bubbled within. The historian knew world history, not to mention Church history, as if he had once lived in those eras long ago. His historical recall was breathtaking; a walking, talking Catholic Encyclopedia from A through Z!

The first night of the class, a beautiful woman with long brunette hair walked in and sat next to me at my table. She appeared to be in her early thirties. Interestingly enough, she looked more like an actress or a model, and I would later find out that she was both during her early twenties. I felt joyful inside to see such a young woman with an interest in Church History. I had a fleeting thought that I'd like to get to know her more.

After class that night we visited while walking to our cars. She told me her name was Vanessa (and I later discovered that the name Vanessa means Butterfly, which is so fitting for her personality). She had been a truth-seeking Evangelical Christian for over 25 years. She fluttered about from Baptist to Presbyterian and everything in between, and now she was seeking a deeper faith experience. Sadly, her 12-year marriage ended in divorce a few months earlier. She knocked on the door of the Catholic Church as she was seeking to gain a deeper biblical understanding of divorce and remarriage. I listened intently to Vanessa, asked further questions about her faith journey, and Vanessa got into my car to continue our visit.

I asked, "Besides the Church teaching on divorce, what else motivated you to investigate the Church?"

With passion and deep conviction, she explained how her love of art and art history inspired her to study the Church architecture and biblically-themed paintings by many Renaissance Catholic artists. When she was a University student, she would spend hours analyzing great works of art and studying the lives of many Catholic artists who were commissioned by the Church to portray biblical events.

Paintings by Baroque-style artist Caravaggio's and his famous work, *The Deposition*, portraying the Blessed Virgin Mary at Christ's side, as well as Michelangelo's famous *Pieta*, profoundly inspired Vanessa to meditate on the death and resurrection of Jesus, as she had never done before, and moved her to come to the class. I was so enthralled by her strong desire to know more about the Catholic faith, and I promised that I would be there to give the appropriate direction whenever she needed it. As a born again Catholic, drawing upon my spiritual building blocks with the religious, my miraculous conversion at the truck stop, and subsequent personal immersion in everything Catholic, I was eager to encourage my new friend, Vanessa, in the Catholic faith. We spoke for almost two hours that evening in my car, and exchanged phone numbers as Vanessa was leaving because we knew this discussion was not over.

Vanessa *Butterfly* would flit in and out of my life for years to come. Eventually, she asked me if I would sponsor her into the faith. I readily accepted and looked forward with great anticipation to the next phase of her adventure. I grew to love her deeply, just like a daughter and eventually a Goddaughter. She had a strong knowledge and a deep love of Jesus from her Protestant roots.

Oftentimes, Vanessa and I would have theological dialogue with our Protestant family and friends, always acknowledging that we have far more in common than not. But most important, in today's society we recognize that we are so blessed to stand shoulder-to-shoulder with our Protestant brothers and sisters in our love of the Lord. What a great joy to share our common ground with each other. Vanessa always walked away from these conversations very inspired to learn more about the Catholic faith.

I felt overjoyed at how the graces of God were working in Vanessa's life. At the root of her newly found faith, Vanessa desired to understand the Body, Blood, Soul and Divinity of Jesus more fully in the Holy Eucharist. She was an eager student and like a butterfly, she would flit from one subject in our faith to another, gracefully, and always full of questions.

She slowly moved from Confession, to Holy Eucharist, to Purgatory, to Blessed Mother, to the Holy Rosary, to the Saints and then back to Purgatory, and then to yet another topic of Catholicism, always desiring to experience and absorb as much of the Church as possible. She would often pray, "Lord I want to believe, help my unbelief."

Over the years, Vanessa and I traveled many roads, pilgrimages, cities, classes, but not without some disputes. With her deep Protestant roots, Vanessa's greatest challenge was the Church teaching about Purgatory. I had no idea Purgatory would bring so much friction and heated discussion between Vanessa and me. It was foreign and contradictory to her Protestant understanding of Heaven and Hell.

In frustration, she would tell me, "I do not understand Purgatory, Teresa. It just does not set well with me."

I gave her books, CDs, and DVDs to help her discover the depth of our Catholic Faith. I spent many tearful and joyful phone hours discussing Purgatory. There were quite a few times when our phone calls would end abruptly with her in tears of frustration, yet she maintained a firm commitment to study and understand the faith. I prayed incessantly for her to be enlightened by the Holy Spirit. I prayed for the grace to be patient in her walk. I knew the Lord sent her to the Church and I was the one He chose to lead her through it. She was eager to become a Catholic even though she fiercely opposed the teaching on Purgatory. Despite her confusion about it, she made a firm decision to register for RCIA at a local Parish in the community.

As her Godmother and sponsor, Vanessa invited me to visit her RCIA class the evening the teacher taught about Purgatory. The RCIA teacher unfortunately did not explain the Church's teaching in a way that inspired Vanessa or the other students. Vanessa asked for my support and insight during the class. I participated as other students had unanswered questions as well.

Thankfully, the RCIA teacher welcomed my involvement, so I shared that more than likely, for most people, Purgatory will be a necessary experience. I asked the class to imagine how one could enter Heaven, as Jesus calls us to be holy, as He is holy in the Bible. "I don't know about you all, but I don't feel as holy as He is calling us to be. The Church has always taught that we have to be purified to that level of holiness, and I want that because if any man's work is burned up he'll suffer loss, but will be saved. God's very essence is love and mercy, and Purgatory would be a person's greatest gift of mercy from their loving Father in Heaven."I want Purgatory if I'm not 100% pure and ready to enter the Kingdom of Heaven.

I explained that through much prayer I came to understand Purgatory as God's Laundromat. After death, we leave here with soiled garments. Depending on how you lived, your garment might only require detergent and a short cycle. On the other hand, your garment might require some pre-wash spot cleaning on stubborn stains, and maybe a longer wash cycle. You may have a garment that requires a pre-soak for several hours with a heavy-duty stain remover before washing. Lastly, you may have a garment that is deeply imbedded with dirt and grime requiring an overnight soak with bleach before washing. The Lord taught me that with the proper cleansing action given to each garment, all the loads would be gloriously clean at the end – fit for a King.

It was breathtaking to observe the truth of Purgatory seeping into Vanessa's soul ever so slowly. Vanessa's understanding of Purgatory became deeper than I could have ever imagined or hoped for as it was in such sharp contrast to her original position. She shared that she was devoutly praying for the Holy Souls in Purgatory. She prays much, offers Masses, and visits cemeteries, sprinkling holy water for the suffering souls. As an artist, Vanessa began to paint the Holy Souls of Purgatory, and I was delighted to see her expressions of love for them through her paintings. They give great tribute and remembrance to these souls. She hopes to encourage others who view her work to intercede and pray for these souls.

While Vanessa was busy learning about the faith, she was also working on her annulment. She announced to me, with extreme independence that "she would do it her way, as fast as possible." Within the first few months of attending the Catholic Church, she met with a Deacon and he was new at his Parish. He learned, along with Vanessa, how the annulment process works.

She quickly contacted people from her past and they agreed in theory to be a witness and fill out the detailed questionnaire.

As the months went by, Vanessa often complained about the annulment process as it seemed so arduous and detailed to her. I reminded her that the Church is there to protect the Sacrament of Marriage, and determine the state of mind of the husband and wife; including all facts related to the dissolution of their marriage. Shortly thereafter, Vanessa received a letter from the Judicial Vicar at the Diocese stating that they had not received the testimony from three of her witnesses. She felt disappointed and upset. In addition, the Deacon helping her in the annulment process, left his position for personal reasons and she found herself without a replacement to guide her through completion.

Two weeks or so after receiving the first upsetting letter, she received more bad news from the Tribunal. The Vicar stated in his second letter that her annulment case "was weak due to lack of witnesses and insufficient evidence for the judges to examine the case and the tribunal judgment would have been a negative decision."

My little butterfly called me immediately with tears flooding her cheeks and with her temper flaring, she exclaimed, "Teresa, I will never become Catholic if my annulment is not granted."

My heart sank as I heard a click on the other end of the phone. I immediately went downstairs to where my husband was sitting at his computer. "Danny, Vanessa just called. Her annulment was pretty much denied. Apparently she did not have enough witness testimonies."

He turned around and said, "Oh, Terri, you'll lose her. She'll never come into the Church unless she gets that annulment."

I replied, "Don't ever say never. I'm going to pray, and remember, she came to the Church and wanted to be a part of it."

I left the room to pray, "Lord, this situation will require a miracle. Could you please undo the Declaration from the Tribunal, if it be your Holy Will?"

Vanessa and I prayed that God would bring her new witnesses to testify on her behalf for her annulment. Vanessa's former husband finally responded to the Diocese, and submitted his witness questionnaire. A friend of Vanessa's for many years knew the pastor that married her. Her friend was a recent convert to Catholicism as well as a University History Professor. After hearing Vanessa's plight, he wrote a letter stating that her former Pastor did not believe that there should be any obstacles to ending a Christian marriage. In fact, her friend provided a cassette tape of a Sunday morning sermon by this pastor stating, *"it was okay to divorce for any reason."*

Eleven months later, Vanessa called me on December 20, 2000, and with tears of joy she screamed, "Teresa I got the annulment! PRAISE GOD! Thank you Jesus!"

I knew in my heart that Vanessa had hopes to remarry someday and it was crucial in her life that she be free to do so in the Catholic Church.

Unexpected Glory.

By the graces of God, Vanessa grew to love all the teachings of Mother Church. I was very privileged to watch a total spiritual paradigm shift of a former Protestant, seeking a fuller faith understanding, to an on-fire Catholic convert. It was miraculous to say the least! There were no more obstacles. Spring of 2002, at the Easter Vigil Mass Vanessa received all the Sacraments of the Catholic Church. The presence of the Holy Spirit was very strong, joyfully welcoming her to the feast of the Holy Eucharist. It was a glorious moment as my darling Goddaughter had now entered fully into the Catholic Church. As she was exiting the Church, the choir was singing the Litany of the Saints, and I felt the presence of all the saints of a 2000-year Christendom.

Vanessa no longer reacted to Catholicism with all its seemingly difficult teachings. She now spoke with joy and loved to share with others about her new found faith. This searching soul was now going to Holy Mass, attending the Blessed Sacrament for adoration; praying the daily Rosary; wearing the blessed medals/scapulars, and even praying novenas. I soon learned that daily Mass was a part of her routine, as well as praying for the souls in Purgatory.

I felt blessed and honored to have played a role in Vanessa's conversion and also in helping her children grow to love the Catholic faith as well. Vanessa soon found a ministry to help the unborn as a champion sidewalk counselor at abortion clinics. She also spreads the fullness of the faith in her local community and when she travels for her work. She is always prepared to give other seeking souls books, CDs, and she is ready to listen with an open heart.

Vanessa has indeed become a *Butterfly for our Lord.* Looking back over these past 18 years, I realize the Hand of God placed us together as His absolute Providence was evident. I received revelations and confirmations of that reality while praying the Holy Rosary. Our Lord wanted me with her in her early Catholic years, until she was safe to fly alone.

In November 2008 on all Saints Day, Vanessa exchanged wedding vows in the Sacrament of Marriage with Craig, a devout Catholic man. They asked my husband and me to be the witnesses at their Nuptial Mass celebrated by Rev. Fr. Louis Marx. She had come full circle, from the sufferings of a divorce, to a joyful marriage in the Catholic Church. Our Lord certainly works all things for good for those who love Him.

Vanessa's wedding in the Catholic Church

Psalm 37

Delight yourself in the Lord;
and He shall give you the desires of your heart.

TWENTY

The Lamb and the Wedding

I was off and running again to find another bible class, as I could not get enough of the Lord's teachings. I called these classes, "Traveling with Jesus and Mary," and I buckled up for the ride because it was thrilling! My children were grown, my husband was well and self sufficient, unlike today, so I took off again in the evening to join a Bible Class in Riverside, California, that I found in my Church bulletin. The class was taught by the brilliant convert lay apologist, Tim Staples, and I was in for a one-of-kind biblical experience, and best of all, a friendship to last a lifetime.

I initially met Tim when he was just beginning to give his personal testimony on cassette tapes. Tim has a gift of transporting you back to biblical days and keeping you on the edge of your seat. His presentation style is so engaging and demonstrative, that you are sad when it's over, as it always seems like you just got started. I would visit with Tim at conferences, after his presentations, and he would share with me his hopes and dreams for the future. He knew he had been gifted with a bountiful grace of a teaching charism, and wanted to follow the Lord's leading wherever it would take him.

Through the years, I prayed for Tim on the petitions he shared with me. I even prayed for the Lord to send him a beautiful wife, as he shared this heartfelt desire with me one night after class. He was so hoping to find a special Catholic woman in which to share his life. Sitting in his classes, I marveled at how the Lord was working in his life. I was there on the sidelines through much of it. I prayed with many people for his health, his future marriage, and his ability to teach as many as possible. Those were marvelous years, as so many desired to learn their faith and understand it through the scriptures.

The intimate nature of Tim's classes always made me feel like we were back in the first centuries, coming together to truly learn the meaning of the scriptures in revealed truth, and in context. The Holy Spirit was moving in Tim, as he traveled to many cities teaching Catholics and giving them a clear under-standing of the sacraments and the Church in the bible. As prayers sometimes get very visible answers, Tim met his amazing future wife, Valerie, at a Blessed Sacrament encounter, as she came in on the wings of an angel. Their engagement journey was shared with many friends and students. We were all a part of this perfect coupling and the wedding invitations arrived with a wedding date set for August 26, 2000.

My precious Goddaughter, Vanessa "Butterfly," offered to drive me to the Church the day of their wedding. As we drove, our sharing of Tim and Valerie was full of joy. Vanessa and I were filled with anticipation and thanksgiving to be able to attend this great event, the Nuptial Mass of Tim and Valerie Staples. Upon arrival we were seated on the left side as guests, and I fervently began to pray, thanking God for all His blessings He was bestowing upon Tim and Valerie. We were a little early so people were silently entering and prayer was filling the church.

Since we were escorted and seated on Valerie's side of the church I could clearly see all of Tim's family on the right side of the church. I didn't know most of them, but it was mentioned during the homily that the presiding priest, Fr. Terry, was Tim's brother. The stories of conversion in Tim's family are astounding. The music was softly filling the church during my prayers of love and hope for the two of them. I became unaware of my surroundings as I went very deep into prayer.

The bride had not yet entered the church when I saw her do so. During a continuum of visions I received while praying, with eyes closed sitting in the church, Valerie walked past me as real as real can be. I came to understand this fact a short while later when she truly did pass me in real time as she walked down the aisle. What I experienced was completely outside of my own thoughts, prayers, understanding and reality.

As I prayed for the bride and groom, scenes enveloped my mind and I became an enraptured spectator. All of the images were moving and lifelike. A marble altar appeared before me with a little lamb as white as snow. The lamb was standing on the altar perpendicular to me with its beautiful face to my left. Drops of brilliant red blood appeared about half way down the Holy Lamb's back and continued in a straight line down to the end of his little tail. I was immediately compelled to worship the Paschal Lamb and my heart swelled with great love. This vision was beyond description.

As the vision continued, I saw Valerie coming down the aisle in my peripheral vision. She was in a stunning, brilliant white wedding gown and there were drops of the same crimson red blood from the back of her waist all the way down the train of her wedding dress to the floor. She was walking very slowly down the aisle towards the altar. During this entire vision, I was infused with the mystical teachings of the Sacrament of Marriage and its relationship to the Passion of Christ on the Cross. The Lord took me to His Passion in a way in which I am struggling to describe. His suffering is embedded deep into the sacraments for us. He gave me an understanding of marriage that was so deep.

Sacramental marriage comes from His side from which blood and water flowed. Marriage is full of sacrificial love, patience and endurance – "until death do we part."

Valerie's wedding gown was the sign of the Sacrament they were about to participate in, before all of Heaven. Spotless and pure, like the Paschal Lamb, offering herself with total self giving – as married love requires extreme selflessness. The crimson-red drops of blood were positioned on her snow white gown, exactly the same as the crimson drops were positioned on the Lamb standing on the Altar. The Precious Blood, shed for all humanity, which is manifested daily in the Eucharistic sacrifice throughout the world, was being revealed in a visual way to me. We must turn to the Lord in total trust in order to endure all the trials that come in a marriage.

This visual experience rendered me to a child-like state of being, where I was in total union with our Eucharistic Lord. Tim and Valerie were going to make their covenant before the Lord on the cross. He gave me the knowledge that Valerie would be an open receptor for Tim's love, a conduit to Almighty God of their fused love, even to the point of the Cross. The Lord also showed me Tim's role, as the bridegroom, emanating a selfless love and a great strength for Valerie, always willing to carry the cross for her and his family, a love that would endure for all eternity. The Sacrament of Marriage is a timeless victory through the suffering and joy of total self giving. I knew I was receiving a great knowledge from the Lord, yet all I could do was watch, weep and receive. It was so intensely Eucharistic in nature that I really could not understand the depth of it all. It transcended all my own understanding, as it was the Knowledge of God, not mine.

The Sacrament of Marriage is so profoundly serious, as its essence is in the Blessed Trinity and the Passion of Christ. The snow white little Lamb with the red drops of blood was the main participant in their wedding. The presiding priest was the instrument of God to proclaim the covenant. The Holy Eucharist is the food and sustenance for the journey. The Pascal Lamb. The Lamb of God who takes away the sins of the world, have mercy upon us. Lamb of God who takes away the sins of the world, grant us peace. Then the vision ended at the sound of glorious wedding music flowing throughout the Church.

I opened my eyes, and in my right peripheral vision I saw Valerie as she was walking down the aisle wearing the gown I saw in the vision, but without the blood droplets upon it. *It was the exact same wedding gown from the vision.*

Unexpected Glory.

All I could do for the entire wedding ceremony was quietly sob, while offering up many prayers for Tim and Valerie with love.

Later when we left, I began to share with Vanessa what I experienced before the wedding, and she pulled her car over and stopped. "Teresa, that is very intense."

She thoughtfully looked down and was trying to absorb it all. I told her that I did not understand much of it either, but I did sense the magnitude of taking the wedding vow before the Lord, the Lamb of God, like never before. I would never view marriage the same way again.

A few months later, I went to San Secondo d'Asti Catholic Church in Ontario, California, to hear Tim teach a class. Valerie was there with him, so I approached them before the class to tell them about the vision. Before I shared with them, Tim smiled when he saw me, and first they both thanked me for my wedding gift, a splendid sculpture of the Last Supper.

I told them of the event at their wedding and they listened intently and Tim remarked, "Wow, how very Biblical and Eucharistic. Truly astonishing."

We looked at each other in awe of the whole thing and Tim excused himself as he had to go teach the class.

I have now been married over 49 years myself and I believe I'm beginning to understand that incredible experience with the Lord, more and more with each day. My own marriage has been an amazing saga of joys, sufferings, extreme difficulties, and triumphs. Without God in my marriage, it would never have survived. I must admit, I have asked the Lord many times since Tim and Valerie's wedding day why He did not give me this incredible knowledge earlier on in my own marriage. The Lord revealed to me that it was His perfect time for me to receive this revelation.

The Lamb of God is far more present in our lives standing on that altar than we could ever imagine. I praise and worship the little snow white Lamb of God. I smile when I recall Tim commenting that my wedding gift representing the Last Supper was amazing given what happened to me at their wedding.

Certainly not a coincidence. I told him that his classes had burst forth with understanding of the biblical Eucharistic discourses. I was led to buy that particular wedding gift because of the fruit of Tim's teachings, which was so appropriate for them, but the vision was far beyond our natural realm. The Lord blessed us all with this great miracle, but Tim would once more have to help me understand it, from a scholarly point of view. I am not a scholar, only a lover of Christ, a willing student, a yielding spirit, and a guest at a magnificent wedding.

Tim and Valerie Staples

Revelations 19:7

Let us rejoice and be glad
And give Him glory.
For the wedding day of the Lamb has come,
His bride has made herself ready.

TWENTY-ONE

Moses and the Blessed Sacrament

In 1996, I had an extraordinary visit from the Holy Spirit requesting me to become a Blessed Sacrament adorer. I really had no idea what that meant, and questioned the Lord as to what He was asking of me. It came on the heels of a two-day retreat during a Charismatic Conference weekend where I was very close with God.

The following weekend I went to Mass at St. Francis de Sales in Riverside, California. In the pew right next to me, I noticed a request form for people to sign up for adoration. I was beyond ecstatic. At that moment, I understood completely the marvelous encounter I had with God the prior weekend. The Lord made sure I saw that little piece of paper. It was no coincidence. The Holy Spirit was instructing me on Holy Hour Devotion and I was learning like a little child because that's about where I was in my faith in 1996.

From the moment of the truck stop miracle, I was rapidly moving through my Catholic catechesis, as the Lord and the Blessed Mother were teaching and guiding me.

I called the Church on Monday and pledged for adoration two days a week, even though I worked 40-50 hours a week in our little business at that time. I committed to be an adorer on Wednesdays at 2:00 p.m. and Sunday mornings at 4:00 a.m., so that I could go right into the 6 a.m. Mass on Sundays with Fr. Louis Marx celebrating the Mass at that time. Father Marx is a holy priest that instituted the 24-hour adoration chapel at St. Frances de Sales Church many years before. I grew to love him with all my heart, and what a great confessor.

I was getting up at 2 a.m. on Sundays, in order to be wide wake to drive to the chapel and make it there by 4:00 a.m. I was able to do the two-day-a-week commitment for a year, but I kept falling asleep in the chapel because I had a deficient thyroid. Eventually, I would cut back to only Wednesdays, but, oh, those 4:00 a.m. mornings. The people I encountered in the chapel, the adoration of Jesus, the pleadings on their knees; I witnessed many demonstrative prayers of people who were in great need of the Lord's mercy, which moved me to tears.

I looked forward all week to those hours with the Lord. Often on Wednesday, there would be a lapse of time before another adorer would arrive, and I would have twenty minutes or so completely alone with Jesus. I used to shut the chapel lights off and sing to the Lord. I had many healings in my heart while in adoration.

There were wounds from my childhood, my marriage, and my personality defects that God slowly healed. I began to reflect inwardly and was healed in many ways, which allowed me to give more freely without expectations from others. I totally yielded to the Holy Spirit, and listened intently to His still, small voice which I heard clearly in the silence while in the chapel. The Lord slowly and gently changed me.

I noticed my temperament mellowing to a much softer me. I had more patience than ever before. God's changes in me are too numerous to recount. I was surprised to find out that we are the ones that need to change. Our happiness does not depend on the world changing, only on the change in us towards the world. I took a lot of pain to the True Presence of Jesus in the Blessed Sacrament for many years. My husband eventually went into remission from alcoholism. My addict son went to prison and was spared from a worse outcome. My daughter and her husband had miraculous conversions and were having lots of babies.

Many people came to me, including Protestants, to discuss the faith and I was witnessing a lot of conversions. I experienced *Great Joy* and *Great Suffering* in my years of adoration in many aspects of life. I had my third grandchild at the same time that I became a prison mom. The adoration hours sustained me accompanied by Holy Mass. I heard Him. I felt Him. I experienced Him. I loved Him. Year after year, I went to adoration in good times, and in bad, in sickness and in health.

In 2001, we moved one hour away from the Blessed Sacrament Chapel, and I could not separate myself from the worship at the chapel. So I continued to drive to Jesus and I knew

He would be pleased. We moved to four acres in the desert of Winchester, California, and we had drilled a well when we developed our property.

In 2007, our water resource from the well began to diminish and slowly trickle out for our needs. Unbeknownst to me, our neighbors above us had their wells go completely dry, which I found out much later, but they had backup county water systems. We did not, and we certainly did not have thousands of dollars to have a meter installed. We began to shut down sprinklers to preserve water, as we had a lot of landscaping. We just had no choice. Every week it got a little drier at our place and I was very concerned about all the fruit trees; we had over 20 of them. I began to really cut back on washing clothes, and our awareness of water was very acute. It became one of our major topics at the dinner table. I had never taken our water shortage into the Blessed Sacrament Chapel as I was continuously overwhelmed with family problems – I barely had time to think about our water problems.

One Wednesday in May of 2007, in the midst of the water crisis, I was busy praying for my husband who was greatly suffering with his leg which was injured years before, and Veterans hospital was talking surgery again. I was also praying for my mother, who was not feeling well at the time – there just was so much to pray about. I'm sure I would have eventually prayed on the well issue that day, but God was way ahead of me. I was praying my heart out in the chapel, profusely loving the Lord, when I heard a beautiful, soft masculine voice.

"Moses, strike the rocks commanding them to bring forth water by the power of the Living God so the people can drink!" I was stunned. I took a deep breath and thanked and thanked the Lord. I was not even thinking of the well, but God knows our every need. I had an understanding of what I was to do.

I went home and told my husband Dan about the words I was given in the chapel, word for word, and then I wrote them down so that I wouldn't forget. I called my dear Catholic friends to help me locate Scriptures that sounded like what I had heard. We discovered it was Exodus and Numbers. In those Scriptures, Moses was the leader with the staff. He was sure having a rough time with those Israelites! After all, there were no fast food places out there in the desert, and his 650,000-person flock were getting really thirsty, hungry and short tempered.

I had an understanding that the Lord wanted me to take the Bible, Holy Water and Blessed Salt down to the well. I was to pray asking for Moses' intercession for water. I sat the Bible at our front door on our end table, and then took off on ice skates in our busy life and forgot about the whole thing again for a week. Of all people, my husband who had just started going to Mass after 40 years of marriage began to ask me if I had been down to the well to pray. I told him I had not had time and he told me to make the time because he was really worried about the well drying up.

Upon Dan's prompting, the next morning I took the Bible, Blessed Salt and Holy Water and walked down the hill to the well house. I stood alone, out amongst the rocks near the well, and began to read Scriptures from Exodus and Numbers out loud, and I found the Scriptures that were very close to what I heard in the Blessed Sacrament Chapel. I called out loud to the Lord in prayer pleading for help with our water, and then I called on Moses. I had a magnificent sense of Mount Tabor where Jesus stood before his apostles emanating the greatest Glory of Light with Moses on one side and Elijah on the other – the Transfiguration! I felt the communion of saints with me.

The patriarchs of old probably don't get a lot of phone calls today from folks crying out for help in these times, but I know my phone call was received. I became aware of his presence; Moses standing right beside me. The whole experience of reading from the Book of the Law with great confidence and love was overwhelming, especially with the knowledge that Moses was right beside me. I felt so much love for him, I cannot even express it.

My entire well area is covered in large and small rocks. The scene is very familiar to the ancient Scriptures, as I live in an area that resembles the Holy Land in many ways; the rocky desert, olive trees, and foothill terrain reminiscent of Mt. Tabor. My arms were up in the air pleading just like Moses did for his army. I felt the power of God in His Saints and my confidence level soared with the eagles. After an hour, or so, I sent love to The Lord and Moses and headed back up to the house. Days later, I mentioned to Dan that the water seemed much more powerful coming out of the faucets. He nodded and off we went into our busy life. Weeks later we realized that our water pressure was back to normal! I knelt down in gratitude thanking Almighty God for His living waters restored on our property, and for the powerful intercession of Moses.

Unexpected Glory.

A few months went by and I went to visit with my Baptist school teacher neighbors who lived behind me. I wanted to take them a gift for the baby boy they had just adopted. The new dad, Gary, was standing at their kitchen table and he blurted out, "So, Terri, when did your well go dry?"

I replied, "Our well did not go dry, has yours?"

He then told me that their well went dry and so did Bob and Ruth's next door to them. He looked very perplexed that Dan and I still had water.

I told him that, "I went to Moses to handle the problem, and we got our water back!"

He then said, "Why Moses, why didn't you go to Jesus?"

I told him, "I did, but Jesus sent me to Moses to bring us water from our rocks."

His wife looked stunned and she said, "Gosh, Gary, you should have gone to Moses!"

A silence came over the kitchen for a moment, and I had the biggest smile inside of me.

As the years went by, I began to refer to him as Uncle Moses. I had such a sense of kinship with him. One day at a Catholic conference, I was admiring statues on a table chatting with the sales lady and out of the blue, she said, "Oh, I have this beautiful statue of Moses in a box under my table that nobody wants!"

I almost fell through the floor and began to tell her the whole story of my well. Needless to say, I walked away with an awesome statue of Moses depicting the Ten Commandments with him striking the rocks with his staff. Unbelievable, and I even got it at a discounted price because nobody wanted to buy Moses at any of the conferences. I love him – my Uncle Moses, and I think my husband loves him, too.

Numbers 20:11

Then, raising his hand, Moses struck the rock
twice with his staff, and water gushed out
in abundance for the community
and their livestock to drink.

TWENTY-TWO

Jesus, I'll Work for You

My daughter Kimberly and her husband Robert (aka, Dr. Robert) had just delivered their seventh child, a boy named Kephas, in a home birth setting. Baby number six, Lily Pearl, was born in their secluded Horse Mountain home in Northern California, since their midwife team couldn't make it physically in time. After much prayer and discernment, Kimberly and Robert along with the phone counsel of the midwife, knew that they needed to continue solo with Lily Pearl. Robert stepped up to the plate, rolled up his sleeves and with Rosary in hand, Lily Pearl was delivered in the middle of the night by her father.

The next morning, when the midwife came to check on both baby and mother, she saw that both of them were in remarkable health. She turned to Robert and congratulated "Dr. Robert" on an amazing home birth. Since that birth #6, Kimberly and Robert have had three more children and they continue with their successful home births. Upon the arrival of #7, a precious tiny boy from Heaven whom they named Kephas, after St. Peter, aka Rocky, I decided to fly up to Northern California and stay several days with Kimberly and family to help her in any way I

199

could while she recovered after birthing Kephas. Kephas is the Aramaic name that Jesus spoke when he renamed Simon Peter.

When I got there, there was so much joy and work to experience. At this point in time, Robert and Kimberly had Malachi, Josiah, Kateri, Chiara, Mirianna, Lily Pearl and Kephas. How blessed I felt to be a grandmother to seven healthy grandchildren. Believe me when I say that there is a great story behind the naming of each child. Seven children, seven blessings from God and this married couple was really living and trusting in Him, as they are totally open to life in their marriage. They live in the providence of the Lord in every way. I played with the children, read to them, rocked babies, did a lot of laundry with Kimberly at the laundromat, thousands of dishes, and enjoyed every moment with my family. Just being together was such a great gift.

When the weekend came during my trip, they took me to Holy Mass and we all thanked St. Joseph for finding them the house they lived in. I was very blessed during my entire trip, spending such focused quality time with them, as we lived so far apart. It was amazing how quickly the days passed, and it was soon time for me to say goodbye and head back to Southern California. Kimberly took me to the airport in Eureka, California, along with all the children in tow. Goodbyes are always so difficult for me. I cry and wonder if I will ever see them again. Financially we were struggling to make ends meet since we had experienced the construction recession, and we certainly couldn't be adding periodic travel expenses to our tight budget.

Once they all left me with goodbye tears at the airport, I approached the scanner to place my suitcase, travel bag and jacket on the belt for clearance. At that moment, I had a very strong prompting to pray, "Lord Jesus, if you have someone on this flight that you would like me to speak with about you, then please, place them next to me on this plane and Jesus, I'll work for you."

Our flight was called to go through the airport scanner and I totally forgot about the little prayer with security procedures going on all around me. Eureka is a small airport and the plane I was getting on was also very small as well, I'm guessing it was a 30-passenger commuter plane with two seats per aisle. I was seated in about the sixth aisle with a man sitting next to me in the window seat. He looked to be around thirty-five years old, and he was wearing glasses, which gave me the impression that he was the intellectual type. I began to pray internally for the flight with deep concentration. I asked St. Michael the Archangel to accompany us with my guardian angel and pleaded with the Blessed Mother to pray for us.

We taxied out onto the tarmac, when the flight attendant came out and announced, "There is a serious technical problem with the plane that must be addressed, therefore you are all to remain in your seats until further notice, as this could take a while. I repeat, stay in your seats," she concluded.

Well, people began chatting all around me as they were trying to figure out what in the world was going on. I looked to my right and smiled at the stranger next to me. "Hi, I guess we are going to be together for a while. My name is Grandma Terri, what's yours?"

He told me his name, unfortunately I never wrote it down and I do not remember what he said, but I will always remember his face, always. I proceeded to tell him about my trip and about all my grandchildren. He then told me he was going to visit his grandmother in San Diego.

I exclaimed, "How wonderful. She is so blessed to have a grandson like you. I can only pray that when my grandsons are older they will come and visit me. I hope my grandsons grow up to be just like you.

At that comment, he got a very strange look on his face and said, "Well, I also have business in Los Angeles to tend to, so it is both a pleasure and business trip for me."

At this juncture, people began to mill about in the aisles of that little plane, trying to stretch a bit, ignoring the flight attendant's strict instructions. I was not about to get up, so the man at the window seat was trapped. I felt myself becoming totally unaware of my surroundings and time seemed to stand still on the plane, as if the stranger and I were the only two people on earth.

I turned to him and said, "So, what kind of business are you in? What do you do for a living?"

He stared at me for a moment with a look I will never forget and replied, "I am a global internet pornography architect."

I stared at him soaking in his words and said, "You are a what? Please repeat that."

And he did. I do not believe I can describe what shot through me, a shock wave bigger than the plane, that I can tell you. I raised my hands up to heaven in the plane and verbally glorified God and thanked Him. I turned to the visibly stunned man after my spirit-filled action and said, "Well, sir, today you have a divine appointment with Jesus Christ! He has sought you out."

There was a brief silence.

Now the boldness of the Holy Spirit began to work through me. My first questions to this man were, "Are you married? Do you have children? Are you baptized, and if so, into what denomination?" I tried to make him feel comfortable with me, asking every question with great love and discernment.

He replied, "I am married with two little girls and was baptized a Lutheran as a very young boy. I was born in Germany."

I responded, "Oh, I see, a Lutheran, well then, you are a baptized Christian. Do you mind, sir, if I tell you what I believe the Lord desires to teach you today?"

He said he did not mind. I silently asked the Holy Spirit to give me what He wanted me to impart to this man who was obviously living a deeply offensive life before God and humanity. I remember feeling like I was in a *"Bubble of Grace"* with him. The

Lord was conducting the entire event, including the delay of the flight.

I began to tell this man about the conversion of St. Paul, the thousands of martyrs, the catacombs, Nero burning Christians displayed as party lamps in the Coliseum, the great danger of attending Mass in the early centuries, the wonders of the True Presence in the Eucharist and the blood spilled by Jesus for the thousands to seed the faith. I explained how the Bible was canonized by the Catholic Church. I spoke of Constantine and all of the Bishops attending his great Council to legalize Christianity. I remember speaking of the Blessed Virgin Mary and the angels and saints. I really focused on the first four centuries intensely taking him at breakneck speed through the Early Church.

The plane began to taxi during my catechism class on the fast track and this gentleman is still trapped at the window seat. His eyes are as big as saucers and he almost looked paralyzed. He had been listening to me for over 90 minutes. I continued on to the first split in Christianity after a thousand years between the East and the West, and I finally made it to Martin Luther. I had total control of the dialog in such a beautiful way since it was the Lord. He was holding that plane in the palm of His Hand on the runway. Literally.

We were still sitting in the plane at the tiny airport in Eureka, California. I began to speak about Luther to him, as he did want to interact on that topic. He asked me a lot of questions and I did my best to answer them. The Holy Spirit was clearly speaking through me, as I seemed able to answer any question he asked me.

We had been moving slowly forward on the tarmacs and we had finally been advised that the technical difficulties had been addressed, and we were preparing for takeoff. As we went up into the heavens, I asked the gentleman next to me if he realized the curse he was bestowing upon his children.

He was stunned, and queried, "A curse?"

I replied, "Yes, a curse. Your children cannot be blessed with your dirty money. Look what God sees you giving millions of people on the internet. I can promise you, if you walk away from what you are doing, the Lord will assist you and bless you. Otherwise, I believe you had this appointment today as a great warning call from God. Do you want your little girls to participate in your industry when they grow up?"

He replied, "Of course not."

I retorted, "Really? Well, that is the legacy you are leaving them both. It is the path you are laying out before them. Can you not see that? Jesus will help you, it will not be easy, you may not make nearly the money you have become accustomed to, but you will have eternal security for you and your family."

A silence fell upon the two of us. I felt a great peace and knew that the Lord's work had been accomplished. We finally landed in Los Angeles and I realized that I just spent well over three hours with a global pornographer, teaching and preaching the Lord Jesus Christ, one-on-one with a man handpicked by Jesus Christ the Lord himself.

Unexpected Glory!

As we prepared to get our carry-ons to get off the plane, I asked him if he would like my phone number. He did not answer me and appeared to run off the plane, but not without the encapsulated catechism teaching of Christendom, and the Lord's dying on the cross for his salvation seared into his soul forever. After all the time on the runway, I must say, there was a change in that man as we flew through the clouds with the angels. His entire countenance had altered from self assuredness to a frightened childlike state. At the end of our flight after arriving at the gate, he ran off that plane and away from me as fast as he could, but he was not the same man that got on the plane. The Lord is so creative. I smiled. No soul is beyond the magnificent mercy of God. Mission accomplished. Jesus, I'll work for you!

Philippians 4:13

I have the strength for everything through him who empowers me.

TWENTY-THREE

The Magnificent Magnificat Meal

Many years ago, I was introduced to a woman named Elissa at a prayer meeting. In retrospect, I cannot fathom the plans of God for all of us that are beyond perfect. Elissa had sixteen years of training – twelve by the Dominicans throughout grade school, and four by the Jesuits throughout college. She and her husband Don have been a pillar of faith for their community, holding prayer meetings, Masses and Rosaries in their home for many years. Their donation of time to their parish has been evident for decades.

Elissa was a teacher of the deaf for the Riverside Unified School District. She had much to share of her knowledge in schooling. So the Lord brought our paths together in the '90s and the sister love was instant. We were both Type C (Catholic) blood types, and we began to fellowship together with other Catholics at retreats, prayer meetings, rosaries, weddings, luncheons and bible classes. I never dreamed that Elissa would someday press on me to write a book.

Many years would pass before that reality would come to fruition. Elissa has a deeply charitable and sweet heart for doing

God's work and is always reaching out to help others in any way she can. My entire family has always felt the great love Elissa has for all of us in so many special ways.

Not too long ago, in the early morning hours before dawn, in preparing for a trip to the VA hospital with my husband, Dan, I had an accident. After assisting Dan into the car with his wheelchair, as I was running back to the house in the dark to get some required paperwork I tripped and fell and broke my ankle. Needless to say, I was the one who went to hospital that day – Dan's visit was put on hold. Thank God no surgery was required, only a cast.

Shortly thereafter, the saints came marching in. It started with my sister Kathryn surprising us with a delicious home cooked meatloaf with all the trimmings. Then my sister Linda drove up with Elissa, carrying in loads of groceries, paper plates, paper cups, lasagna, and salads, with Elissa's son, John, generously contributing to the abundance and many delights to last us for weeks. They really set us up for the long haul. The love, the assistance, the thoughtfulness, compassion and prayers helped us get through that challenging ordeal.

I was overwhelmed with their kindness. With both of us sitting there in wheelchairs on Thanksgiving Day, my sister Linda brought in the dinner saying, "Boy, you two give a whole new meaning to meals on wheels!"

Our local chapter of the Knights of Columbus, Council 7846, from St. Vincent Ferrer in Sun City also came marching in.

Knight "Shorty" brought us a delicious meal, and Knight Jimmy Duke offered the help from the Knights in any capacity we might need during my recovery. In addition, parishioners Tony and Carmen had heard that I was crawling around inside my home because the wheelchair was man's wheelchair, too big for me. The next thing I knew, they were at my door with a small ladies mobility scooter. What would I have done without the help of all my sisters and brothers in Christ.

A few years ago, Elissa invited me to a breakfast called "The Magnificat Meal" which included breakfast, special speakers and Catholic ministry. The event would take place in Orange County, California, under the direction of Kathleen Beckman along with a group of very gifted Catholic women. They regularly host this fantastic brunch speaker meeting with dedicated guests. Kathleen Beckman is a highly anointed lay prayer leader of the Magnificat Meal of which I felt very privileged to attend. We were so blessed with the priestly presence of Father Raymond Skonezny, who is always dressed in his clerical attire — no matter what the affair. Father Ray proceeded to say the prayer that morning over the meal and the anointing began. I had attended these "meals" before in past years and always felt the presence of the Holy Spirit.

This particular day, Elissa asked me if I could be the door greeter. "Yes, dear Elissa, I would love to participate, just show me what you want me to do," I replied. I was thrilled. Elissa led me out to the hallway of the hotel and told me to greet every person and make them feel welcome. As I stood there, I remembered the other wonderful Magnificat Meals I had attended through the years and the marvelous spiritual happenings that occurred to me and my family members. I warmly welcomed many ladies with the love of Christ, and during the hugs, I did not notice that my glasses fell down and were hanging by the chain around my neck. I just got so wrapped up in loving every person who I did not notice that I could not see them very well.

Way down at the end of the hallway, I saw three ladies heading my way. The one in the middle looked like Esperanza, "Essie," the lady that called Ron, Judy and me the Rising Catholics (Glory Seven). Whenever I would see Essie at an event, she would tease me and say, "I don't want to talk to you. You never call me back. I keep giving you my phone number and then two years later I see you again, and you still have never called me."

I would always tell her, "Oh, Essie, dear, if you only knew. I live a very demanding lifestyle consumed with my husband, his business, grandkids, my son and daughter and their families, as well as other extended family members. Please forgive me."

Anyway, I really cared about this lady, Essie. I would have loved to have spent more time with her throughout the years, but we lived far apart, more than a couple hours, so it just never happened.

As the three women got closer, I thought for certain it was Essie, and she was really going to be mad at me this time. I knew she gave me her phone number over a year ago, and I still had not had the time to call her. I was really in trouble. I was going to have to give her the greeting of all greetings and make her feel welcomed and loved. I began to jump up and down, twirl around, raise my hands up in joy, and squealed, "ESSIE, ESSIE!"

I did this over and over as these ladies made their way to me at the door. I must have looked like a complete nut to them jumping up and down in that hallway. Hilarious, I am sure. I continued these antics until they got up close enough to where I could see it was not Essie! I did not realize fully what a difference your glasses could make until that very moment.

They walked up and said, "Are you alright?"

I was speechless for a change. I had put my glasses back on and I stuttered, "Uh, I thought you were Essie."

They said, "Essie, who's Essie?"

I told them that she was someone I had not seen for a while and wanted to make sure I made her feel very welcome.

They said, "Really, well you sure made us feel welcome!"

They were laughing their heads off as they went into the banquet room and I could still hear their peals of laughter and comments about the whole thing as they were being seated.

When my door greeting duties were fulfilled, I went to my assigned table and noticed I did not know any of the women that were seated with me, so I introduced myself. Well, the really funny part about this was that Essie never came to that particular luncheon, even though she was a part of the Orange County Magnificat Chapter. My unique greeting technique had a lot of people laughing, and it certainly brought an aura of love and joy into that general area.

At that time, we were called by Kathleen Beckman to pray the Rosary. Apparently, the Magnificat participants always pray The Visitation decade of the Joyful Mystery as each event begins. We all pulled out our rosaries and began to pray. Kathleen has many beautiful gifts of leading others into powerful prayer journeys. She is a great instrument for the Lord. She led, and I fell deeply into the rosary prayer. I was focusing on the mystery we were praying where Holy Mother Mary is visiting with her older cousin Elizabeth. Our Blessed Mother was making her pilgrimage in the heat, all those many miles by donkey, to get to her cousin in order to support her in her pregnancy.

I was absorbed in the whole scene where Elizabeth exclaims to Mary how blessed she was to be paid a visit by the Mother of her Lord. Elizabeth was showing Mary great veneration in The Visitation. I was thinking about little John the Baptist and the baby Jesus – both in the womb – one leaping with great joy to the other – certainly one-of-a-kind cousins. About halfway through the decade I heard the most beautiful, gentle, kind, sweet, feminine voice audibly speak a compassionate command into my right ear, *"That is the way I want all of you to be with everyone."*

Unexpected Glory.

In the middle of decade, I heard Our Lady say clearly to me that we should all be the way I was in the hallway with everyone.

At the very least, reaching out and loving all people and making them feel welcome.

I began to cry so hard that I had to get up and leave the table and go to the ladies room to get some tissues, before the Rosary had ended. I sat on a little sofa in the ladies room at the hotel sobbing. A woman came in and said, "Are you alright, dear?"

I told her that the Blessed Mother had just told me we must love and serve all people with a very great outpouring of self. I was so visibly shook up that she just stood by me with her hand on my shoulder for a while. It was a deeply spiritual period of time. I was rendered motionless by the entire event. As I continued to sob, with the woman at my side, I asked Our Blessed Mother, "Is that the way you want me to be when I shop at Stater Bros., Home Depot, or when at the bank, with strangers, everybody?" I continued to weep in the ladies room. I was able to return to the table about thirty minutes later, and I knew I would never be the same.

I always had a great love for people, but that would now be taken to an entirely new level. I began to understand the type of love Our Lady spoke of, and how it heals all wounds. It is love without condition - unconditional love for *all* humanity. It is love with complete trust in God during desperate situations. It seeds the hearts around us with peace, gentleness, kindness, understanding, and patience. There is never divisiveness with the type of love Our Lady put upon my heart during the locution.

She wants us to love *all* people as the entire human race was created by the same God. Jesus is our older brother, therefore, the Blessed Virgin Mary is the Mother of all humanity.

I returned home after the Magnificat Meal after having my socks blessed off by the Blessed Virgin Mary, and I couldn't wait to journey out and experience my new mission. My first public encounter was grocery shopping at Stater Bros. I found myself extremely animated in my actions – greeting everyone with smiles and "hellos," trying to pray a Hail Mary for each and every person I saw in the store while pushing my cart. I quickly learned that I couldn't get through my shopping as I was too busy praying for everyone.

When I finally got up to the checkout counter I noticed the person behind me had a lot less items than me, so I told them to go ahead of me with a big smile. They were thrilled! Then I noticed the next person also had less, so I told them to go in front of me. This went on for three or four people until the checker started laughing and told me to come on up and get checked out. All the people in that area were very happy that someone would send everyone ahead of them in the line. In the future, I would pray one Hail Mary for everyone in the market in order to get my shopping done!

A few days later, I found myself doing the same animated behavior at the bank and Home Depot. I was smiling and greeting everyone I met! This outpouring of love to the people I encountered gave me great joy, and it seemed to cultivate change in others around me. People were praying with me in parking lots; at Target; at the produce department. I was praying for the waiter or waitress at a restaurant, but most especially the bus boy - the one that would normally be ignored. From the doctor's office, to the schools, to the clients I worked with - everyone in my path was getting a prayer. I was not physically jumping for joy, like I did initially as a greeter at the Magnificat Meal, but I was extending God's love to everyone, in little ways, everywhere.

Well, Essie never did show up for the Magnificat Meal, but her presence was with me all throughout the heavenly encounter with the Blessed Mother. The thought of seeing Essie stimulated a welcome response from me that seemingly got the attention of Jesus and Mary. I will always be grateful to Essie for my profound teaching that day, *"That is the way I want all of you to be with everyone."*

My dear friend, Essie

John 13: 34

I give you a new commandment:
Love one another.
As I have loved you,
so you also should love one another.

TWENTY FOUR

The Passover and the Crucifix

One day, my dear sister in the Lord, Elissa, called me with a prayer petition for her son, John. She told me his situation and asked me to pray for him. She wanted to stand at Heaven's Gate to plead for her son who had a very burdensome land deal that was bringing him great pressure and grief. I then asked her if she would like to do a nine-day novena to Our Lady of Perpetual Help for this particular dire financial situation. She was very happy to have a prayer partner come forth to support her and we set our date to begin. What joy our Blessed Mother can bring; spending time with The Blessed Virgin Mary is one of the great gifts of being a Catholic.

Elissa once gave my mother, Lillian, a beautiful surprise birthday luncheon, serving us an elegant meal, with the greatest love and attention. I remember how I felt as she showered Lillian with such honor and recognition. I knew how much Elissa loved me, by her demonstration of joy-filled love upon my own mother. Lillian was so happy that she welled up with tears overwhelmed by all the attention. It must bring Jesus great joy when we go to His Mother with such love and veneration. It is humanly impossible for us to understand the love between the Messiah and the Virgin Mother.

Elissa is known in our community as being a leader of prayer groups, corporal works of mercy at hospitals; praying for the sick and dying; and celebrating Holy Days in her own home with large groups displaying her charitable heart with amazing organization and event planning expertise. She is such a good daughter in celebrating September 8th every year with a birthday party for Our Blessed Mother.

Just the anticipation of the upcoming novena to Our Lady of Perpetual Help brought a sense of great hope to Elissa and John. This was during the crux of the Great Recession of 2008 and Elissa's son was experiencing a very painful blow from the real estate market and suffering greatly. The beautiful image of Our Lady of Perpetual Help was first placed in the Church of San Matteo in Rome in 1499. The image was thought to be lost at one point after Napoleon's armies sacked the Cathedral in 1798.

Thanks be to God, it was actually in the care of the Augustinian fathers until Pope Pius 1X mandated that the icon be given to the Redemptorist order at the Church of St. Alphonsus in Rome in 1866 for public viewing once again. Since that time prints have been placed in churches all over the world. In this famous icon, Jesus is safely cradled in his mother's arms looking with anxiety at St. Gabriel the Archangel, who holds the cross and nails for His Crucifixion. St. Michael the Archangel, at left, holds the lance, spear and the vessel of vinegar and gall for the future Passion of our Lord as well. The Blessed Mother looks at us very solemnly, as if in contemplation of her beloved Son's coming Passion and death for our salvation. Our Blessed Mother never intercedes for anything contrary to the Will of God.

Elissa and me celebrating the Blessed Mother's Birthday

We felt a very strong pull towards that icon for John who needed great intercession, so we began our Rosary novena in the evenings. For nine consecutive nights, we would pray the Rosary together on the phone, and it seemed like the hour flew being immersed in God's grace. Towards the end of that hour, on what I believe was the eighth day of the novena, we were about halfway through the Rosary when an incredible image came into my mind, without any forethought. We had been praying our petition before each Hail Mary when I clearly saw rolling hills of a sort, with a more prominent hill in the middle.

There in front of my mind's eye was a very large wooden cross with a huge carved corpus on it. The crucifix was on the middle of three rolling hills, and was beckoning me to pray with eyes affixed upon it. I gasped internally, as it stayed with me for the remaining decade of the Rosary that night. When Elissa and I were completely done with the Holy Rosary I told her what I had seen. She asked me if I had an understanding of the vision.

I told her, "Not really, but I know that our beloved John whom we are praying for must keep his eyes on the Cross," - that much I understood.

And the same applies to us. It was clear to me on a deeper level that oftentimes trials are a part of our journey here on earth, necessary for our own spiritual growth. The Crucifix before us gives us the strength and perseverance to forge on uphill. Keep your eyes on the Cross. What a beautiful message I received that night. Even though I had loved the Cross immensely since the truck stop miracle, I received even more lights on it that evening.

Elissa was soft spoken and very reverent about it when she said, "My Teresa, what a beautiful sight that must have been to behold. I wonder what the Lord has in store for John as a result of our Rosary?"

Time passed by, and life moved slowly during the great recession. Jobs were disappearing everywhere; homes were being vacated; families were suffering with no relief in sight. Elissa eventually set up a visit for me at John's house. When the three of us gathered at his home, we first discussed the vision I received during the Rosary novena. I remember clearly, sitting there telling John what I saw in our contemplative discussion.

He looked at me and said, "Teresa, what do you think the Lord was telling you in the Rosary novena that night?"

I told him there was not a clearly defined message with the vision, but I was imbued deeply to gaze upon Our Savior on the crucifix with great love and thanksgiving for His Sacrifice for us. We can be assured He will assist and comfort us while we carry our personal crosses uphill. I told him I, too, had deeply felt the recession in our business as well. Danny and I were way down on income and were cutting corners in every direction to make ends meet.

My husband was now in a wheelchair and life was changing rapidly. Just knowing that Our Redeemer is with us, sustains us. I told John that I felt the three of us were standing at the Cross that night in the prayers of the Rosary novena, just staring up at Him with the all the love coming to us from the Holy Spirit. The images before me were very still and rather dark and cloudy, as we were not in the sunlight in the vision. The three of us really enjoyed our visit and when we parted I would not see John again for quite a while.

Several weeks later, I received a phone call from Elissa insisting I go with her to a Passover dinner at her Church. She wanted to buy me a ticket for the dinner and needed to be sure I could attend. Elissa and I always had such marvelous times together. I was full of joy over being invited. The evening came and I drove to the Church. What a beautiful event. There was a Rabbi and a Catholic priest at the head table with some other people. They read Old Testament Scriptures to tell the Passover story.

The readings took us back in time and we were emotionally experiencing the Passover that evening with Moses' people. We were served the delicious Passover meal, in courses, throughout the night. The sharing of the food, scripture and fellowship at each table was very binding upon all of us. I loved every moment. Elissa and I were listening closely to the scripture readings, then remembering the Passover Flight and experiencing great gratitude to God for freeing His People. Elissa was intent on my evening being a shared joy between the two of us. We were so happy to be together and at times leaned over to hug one another with expression of silent love.

As the evening was coming to a close, she reached over to me and said, "Teresa, I want you to follow me somewhere tonight for about a half hour, and then you can drive home. Do not ask me why. It is a surprise."

She had quite a gleam in her eyes. I replied, "Well, alright, but remember, my night driving isn't the best and I have got to take the freeway home."

She agreed, but reminded me I had my prescription glasses she had gifted me, therefore, no worries. So off we went into the night. I followed her to a point, when she pulled over and parked in a residential area and told me to get into her car. I hopped in and off we went, like two school girls heading off for an adventure. She was bubbling over with her secret surprise in the car. She began to climb up into a hilly area with very nice homes.

We were now silent in the car as we drove the windy road up to a type of asphalt hill and as I looked off to the left, I was astounded, there were the hills I had seen in the Rosary novena vision weeks earlier, and there was the same giant wooden crucifix with lights shining upon it! Jesus was profoundly visual on that Cross. The wood Crucifix was simply exquisite.

I gasped, Elissa, "That is exactly what I saw in my vision the night of our Rosary novena."

She said, "I know Teresa."

We parked, got out of the car, and just stared at the sight before us enveloped by stars. A great silence cloaked us, out there that night as we stared at the Savior on the giant Cross on the hill. I was overwhelmed. Tears began to flow. Where was I? Oh, Dear God, I was within eye's view of John's house - I could see it in the distance. He could see the Cross from the window of his home.

Unexpected Glory.

Elissa and I just stood there in God's grace and knew we were witnessing a profound miracle. She told me that the Cross had been erected after the Rosary novena vision. It was erected on the property of John's neighbors. John knew that his neighbors, Jerry and Leona, had purchased the cross about a month or so after the Rosary novena! So John put a plan in place to discover the details of the cross from his neighbors.

Eventually, by the grace of God, the neighbors invited us to their secluded property to walk up the hill to the Crucifix and pray. Jerry and Leona were delighted to hear the story of my vision of their Crucifix. I just marvel at how the Lord of Hosts puts things in place, according to His will. Elissa, her son, John, my grandson Malachi, my sister Linda, and I went on this journey together to visit the Crucifix. What a journey to experience such a miracle as *pilgrims*. We prayed the Chaplet of Divine Mercy up on the hill, and then sat in silence in awe of His perfect sacrifice.

We listened as Jerry and Leona told us of this incredible acquisition. They had taken a trip to Las Vegas shortly before the Passover dinner that Elissa and I had recently attended. Apparently they were on their way home and Leona wanted to stop at a huge pottery and fountain yard in the desert to purchase a fountain. Once they stopped, Jerry was invited by the owner of the yard into a large plane hangar to see other items he had for sale.

He showed Jerry the Crucifix, of which he actually had two, and told him, "Nobody seems interested in this type of thing anymore," and wondered if he would like to buy one. Jerry was ecstatic, and purchased it on the spot, as he himself loves carving wooden crosses. Jerry strapped it onto the top of his truck and drove it home from Las Vegas. The passersby on the highway were awestruck by the sight of this huge Crucifix traveling down the freeway.

One of Linda's incredible pictures which
captures the beauty of this Crucifix

Linda took many photos of all of us on the hill that day as the group visited the Crucifix. She wanted to capture the beauty of that contemplative afternoon, but was completely unaware of the miraculous events behind the great Crucifix vision, as I had not yet shared it with her. The Holy Spirit guided her camera lens as only He can do. She took the photos during the afternoon sunset that day with no idea they would eventually be used in this remarkable story. At that time, I didn't even know I was going to write a book.

Jerry had help erecting the Crucifix with custom cable and lighting in order for it to be visible at night as he always wanted it to be seen by anyone who was in area. Absolutely stunning. They had no idea when they purchased the Crucifix that they were acting upon the Holy Spirit's prompting in a mighty way.

Jerry and Leona were very open and gracious to the Catholic pilgrimage coming to their home. They couldn't have been more hospitable. It's so amazing how God works. He gave the task of securing a carved wooden Crucifix in another state to a Protestant man who had been carving crosses for many years. Jerry even offered to carve Romanesque-type park benches up near the cross so that people who come to pray can rest and have the time they need for contemplative prayer. We began to go over there occasionally and pray.

The years went by and John's financial storms began to calm considerably. As the dark days passed, John kept his eyes affixed on the Crucifix, as he saw it every day from his window.

Jesus Christ was his anchor, and the Blessed Mother was his comfort. Many blessings came to John over a period of several years. His phenomenal building skills are now back at work. He is also doing great things for the Church - Praise be to God.

My hope is to visit Jerry and Leona again soon, and pray with them up on the hill - from the Passover to the Crucifix.

Matthew 16:24

Then Jesus said to his disciples,
"Whoever wishes to come after me
must deny himself,
take up his cross and follow me."

TWENTY-FIVE

Is This What I was Born For?

My desert home and surroundings were very peaceful in Winchester, California. It is so quiet on my four acres that you can hear bird songs and critter noises throughout the day which creates a serene and contemplative atmosphere for prayer. I held to fasting on Wednesdays and Fridays for years, but it became more difficult as I got older. I would get pretty weak and tired, so I adjusted my love offering to the Lord, by fasting only on Wednesdays. I juggled my work hours in Dan's little business which was shrinking every year, so I could continue to go to the Blessed Sacrament Chapel on my fasting day.

The time spent with Jesus in the Blessed Sacrament was always so healing and miraculous. Even though I had moved to a more remote location, I looked forward to going and being blessed by the Savior each week. I sometimes went while very distraught, in bad weather, in illness, in exhaustion, in sorrow, in grief, in pleadings, in shock, never failing to be healed while in the chapel. At times, when in the chapel, I was so ill with my thyroid I would find myself falling asleep while sitting up.

During a prayer for one of my dear friends, Ramona, a mother of three, who suffered from M.S., I fell asleep and the Blessed Mother came to me in a dream. As I was coming out of a deep sleep, I saw the Blessed Mother's lovely profile. Her hands were clasped upward in a solemn attitude of prayer. I fell asleep praying for a mother, and slowly awakened to Our Holy Mother, while sitting right in front of Jesus. I can attest that the Blessed Sacrament is a place where the soul meets God.

Sometimes I would go to the chapel very weak and faint from fasting, and by the time I left, I had a supernatural strength for the long drive home in traffic. I was able to work on our property when I got back, and still make dinner for Dan. On one very traumatic occasion I remember going to the chapel and falling on my knees saying, "Dear Lord, this suffering is so great in my heart, can You even help me today? I believe it is slowly killing me, this pain with my loved one. It is too great. Please forgive my lack of trust and heal me of it.

After thirty minutes in the Blessed Sacrament, deeply loving the Lord, I was trying to remember the problem I had when I entered the chapel. He melted it away and filled my heart with so much love for Him and everyone else, that I could not remember what I crawled in lamenting about. The Blessed Sacrament. A place of God's Wonder and Healing. Oh, how I love my time in the chapel. I know I do not realize the graces I have received from the many years spent in the Blessed Sacrament. Someday they will be revealed to me, but I can tell you that they are great.

One day after my Holy Hour at the chapel while driving home, I remembered that I needed to take out the trash. We had accumulated a lot of hefty trash bags, and they needed to be walked out a ways down a dirt road to our large dumpster. My husband was on crutches and it had become difficult for him to help since his injury. Upon arriving home, and still pretty weak from fasting, I picked up one of the large hefty bags and heaved it up and over my shoulder and headed out to the porch. Dan was out on the porch smoking, and as I walked behind him he blew a bunch of smoke out and it drifted back directly into my face. I was aghast by the smoke and gagged. It was awful to breathe it, especially with the fasting.

As I continued my walk alone to the dumpster I cried out, "Oh, God, is this what I was born for?" I continued to carry the large, heavy trash bag over my shoulder for about 75 feet to the dumpster bemoaning the cigarette smoke incident. It really turned my stomach and I was exhausted and feeling sorry for myself. I was almost to the dumpster when I began to reflect on my crying out to the Lord.

What a moment. As I went through our property gates and finally made my way to the dumpster, I began to speak out loud to Almighty God in the quiet of the desert. "Oh Lord, can you forgive me for complaining? I must have sounded like the Israelites with Moses. Complain, complain, complain. I know I am related in some way to them, that's for sure, but I am very sorry for not just picking up my cross and carrying it. I love you so much, please forgive me."

Well, that was that. I went back to the house and forgot all about it. This was in early June of 2007. The walk to the dumpster happened on a Wednesday. Sunday came, and off we went to Mass. My husband had just begun attending Mass in January of that same year after 42 years of marriage. The Lord was slowly bringing in the sheep of our family back into His fold. The Mass was magnificent as always, but I did not notice anything unusual. When you enter into the Mass, you always experience the bountiful Banquet of the Lamb, but the next Sunday would be life changing for me.

When going up to receive the Lord I bowed gently from the waist behind the person in front of me receiving communion. I was praising and loving Him. As I approached the Eucharistic minister, I suddenly became aware of a very large, maybe 10' tall figure, looming down from above, right at the altar's edge, swooping close to my right ear. I seemed to be gifted at that moment with an acute sensory perception of The Unseen and It's every movement. I also knew the figure was wearing a robe of some kind. Then, this most Awesome Being came down to my right ear and softly said, "Noooooo, *THIS* is what you were born for!" The word NO was spoken very slowly and drawn out.

Unexpected Glory.

I gasped and almost ran from the altar. I was stunned. My response was that of a child. "Oh Lord, you're scary, you hear everything."I was so startled and my emotions were running all over the place. Jesus just told me that I was born to receive Him in the Eucharist. But my first response was embarrassment that He really, truly does hear every word we say. I knew it in my head, but now I knew it because He told me so. "Oh God, is this what I was born for?"

Then, eleven days later, "No, this is what you were born for." He waited a week and a half to let me know that not only does He hear everything, He remembers everything, as I had forgotten the incident altogether. He orchestrates events in our lives with great masterful perfection.

As the months flew by, I would meditate and pray on those words. I knew that marriage, children, family, work in all its different facets, cooking, playing the piano, helping others in many different ways – all these things were what I thought I was born to do, but the words that He spoke to me at Mass were the words of Eternal Life. Now I knew why I was sprinting to the Church after the truck stop miracle. This union between God and human is the greatest miracle possible on earth. The intimacy you experience during the precious moments with Christ's Body and precious Blood in the Holy Eucharist is the greatest gift from God while we are sojourning through life on Earth. Only an Omniscient Eternal Genius could have created such a gift.

I could not get Jesus, and those moments at the altar, out of my mind. I wanted to tell everybody about it. It is so difficult to communicate, even to those close to me, as I cannot *give* them the experience. I can *only tell them* what I experienced at St. Vincent's Catholic Church on that blessed day. The same Jesus is giving himself to millions of souls all over the world at every Mass.

Jesus is with us in everything we do, but during Holy Mass when we receive Him in the Most Holy Eucharist, His Body is intimate with our flesh and our every cell, His Precious blood commingles with ours. For a short period of time, we have God within us exploding throughout our systems, with His Love and Healing – the union that God desires with us, a merged union of the Creator and His Creation. I slowly began to understand the words of Jesus to me that day. It became clear to me that in the future, in another passage of my life, I will spend a great deal of time at Holy Mass. Every Sunday I stare up for a moment at the altar ceiling, and I remember Jesus speaking directly into my ear. I pray that upon my final breath here on earth I will hear in my ear the words, "The Body of Christ."

1 Corinthians 11:27

Therefore, whoever eats the bread
or drinks the cup of the Lord unworthily
will have to answer for the
body and blood of the Lord.

The Praetorium

As the years flew by, I had many mystical experiences during the Mass. I was a participant in the Heavenly Banquet, the greatest event on earth, oblivious to any earthly concerns during that blessed hour. Once I entered the Catholic Church doors, I left all earthly concerns behind. I want to share other delights of the Eucharist that came fleeting through my soul during the Mass.

❖ Once after receiving the Eucharist on my tongue, as I was walking back to my seat, the Host melted inside my mouth very delightfully tasting of honey. What a beautiful surprise.

❖ Another time, as I knelt down to pray, with the Eucharist melting in my mouth as I virtually always take and eat very slowly, with eyes closed, I beheld a vision of blue skies in heaven, surrounded by fluffy white clouds in my mind's eye. I was camel spinning in heaven on ice skates with my arms raised up praising God. I was full of extreme joy praising the Lord, spinning like a top. A beautiful sight, a view into my future, I pray.

❖ At another Mass, I heard the words, "Degeneration of Veneration," upon kneeling with the Eucharistic Lord within me. I was with my daughter, Kimberly and her husband Robert at a Mass at St. Christopher's Church in Moreno Valley, California in 1994, and I shared it with them when we walked out after Mass. I understood it to mean that things would get much worse in the world.

❖ One day I was at Mass at my present Church, St. Vincent Ferrer in Sun City, California, with my daughter Kimberly, who had recently experienced a tremendous upset with someone she deeply cared about. Some time had passed since the incident, so she believed she was at peace with the situation and had pretty much forgotten about it, so she thought.

Apparently, as we knelt down to pray upon reception of Our Lord, Kimberly began to have a vision, kneeling next to me. She asked the Lord Jesus if He would forgive her for losing her patience and her temper with her children, and prayed that He would give her the grace to always love them like she did when she gazed upon them sleeping. She received her answer. He spoke to her internally, "Yes, I will forgive you, Kimberly, if you will forgive this one and love her, like when she is sleeping."

Kim was then shown the person she had been upset with, sleeping peacefully on a great big beautiful bed. Oh Dear Lord, when we got out into the front of the Church, she told me what happened to her during Mass and was gently trembling and crying. She knew through the miracle during

Holy Communion that she had not completely forgiven the person she was shown.

I exclaimed, "Speak Lord, your servants are listening," and began to cry, too. I was full of joy that she received a personal teaching from Jesus, in exactly the same style He used when He walked with the apostles.

What an impact on how we interact with others and are called to forgive. I was so full of joy for my daughter experiencing such a miracle at Holy Mass. This teaching was deep. It reached way down into our souls and stayed. We knew it was Him and considered the whole event to be a very great honor for Kimberly to have such a vision at Mass. I was affected as though I too, had seen and heard the whole thing and that was The Lord's Hand upon us both. I have been very blessed throughout the years to receive other Eucharistic miracles with Kimberly and her husband Robert as our journey together progressed. There were a number of them that I journalized, but I wanted to share a few of them here, before I take you to one that was a great revelation for all of us, possibly unknown.

Again, at my church years later, during Lent, I was deeply praying during the Liturgy of the Eucharist and meditating on Christ's Love for all of us. I have no forethought of seeing or hearing such things when this type of event happens to me. It just simply begins and I am perfectly still and open to God without reservations of any kind, just a child before the Lord.

❖ One morning at Mass, a deathly quiet took over all my senses. It was after I received Him in the Eucharist. I no longer was aware of any external sounds, music, movement – nothing. After receiving the Eucharist and kneeling in prayer in the pew, with my eyes closed, I experienced a living, moving event in my mind's eyes, just like in reality.

The first thing I saw looked like four giant pillars holding up a roof in a grayish, gloomy place. The open-air building looked to be Romanesque in architecture. There were no other buildings, people or cities surrounding this area. There were no walls, as the area was open on all sides, and the scene before me was just this place of great suffering. In the center was another very large pillar reaching to the roof. Our Lord Jesus was bound to the center large pillar, kind of hunched over hugging it very, very weak.

There were three Roman soldiers with huge whips that began beating Him in front of me. These whips had some sort of metal type little spikes coming out of them; it was terrible. Their hatred for Jesus was raging into my mind and heart. They were striping Him viciously, and tiny bits of His flesh and blood were flying off Our Lord and then gracefully soaring out of this Praetorium-type building into the universe.

As these tiny pieces of His Body and Blood projected out, I was then shown multitudes of faces out in the universe waiting. I only saw their faces, necks and shoulders, no hair, and they exuded a Peace that is indescribable. They were everywhere in the open air of the massive universe. The silence, if only I could express the silence in all of this. It was deafening.

I then heard a voice, "These are my eternal people." Then, beyond any comprehension, the tiny bits of flesh became little Eucharists. I watched His Flesh and Blood transform as it flew through space and the faces then tipped their heads back and stuck out their tongues with the greatest reverence. The little Eucharists were landing on thousands of tongues with His Heavenly Peace emanating throughout the universe. *Unexpected Glory.*

Again, the silence in all of this could only have been from Almighty God. The soldiers continued to stripe our Jesus without mercy. He sank into the pillar with so much weakness and submission for our salvation. I watched in rapt attention as this scene unfolded, amazed at Our Lord's Body and Blood becoming food for all ages at the pillar.

I then saw these words in very large letters below the Praetorium that appeared for me to read, "Whoever eats My flesh and drinks My blood remains in Me and I in him." What a privilege to be shown this event that happened two thousand years ago in a very different way. The Paschal Lamb feeding souls eternally right in front of me. I will never be able to describe the effect of these scenes shown to me. When it was all over I sank into the pew, weak from witnessing it all. I could not fully comprehend most of what I saw.

As the weeks went by, I prayed for more understanding from the Lord. I had a knowing that Jesus Flesh and Blood sacrificed at that Pillar during the scourging is where transubstantiation really began. God is so far beyond our understanding, after all, the Eucharist was all His glorious idea in the first place. I do not pretend to understand His ways, I only know what I saw was the truth. He has given authority to His Priests to consecrate the Eucharist into His Body and Blood, but the power will always remain His to make it happen. It is God Almighty who gives the creative miracle of the consecration of bread and wine by our priests in order to feed the Body of Christ on our altars throughout the world.

Answering the call, to become a Catholic priest is a huge responsibility before God. Imagine standing in front of Jesus with hundreds of souls behind Him with their heads tilted back waiting for the Eucharist that you just consecrated. The priest is a part of that wonderful mystery in salvation history. I hope and pray many priests read this and fall to the ground in thanksgiving for their vocation. Each priest is serving their Creator's desire to feed His children by His own personal design. I will always see, upon reflection, that very gloomy, grayish scene of torture and feel a great sense of remorse for my own sins that contributed to that blood splattered pillar.

Yet, Jesus left a sacramental staircase for us to climb during our lives, always looking up to Him with great hope in His mercy, forgiveness and compassion. He beckons us to humility and holiness. Contrite hearts, confession, reparation and then the angel food for the journey. Can a great Father do more for His children? He gives us the subsistence we need for our own personal journey and the wisdom through the sacraments to navigate very dangerous paths. He heals us of many spiritual and physical ailments in His own time and way, when we receive Him in the Eucharist. Daily communicants oftentimes seem to radiate a sort of light from God. He beckons us in the Bible to eat His Body and Blood, and makes us accountable for it.

Oh, thank you, Dear Lord, for this great gift of our priests and the Holy Eucharist. I pray for all to receive the gift of believing in the True Presence of the Holy Eucharist, as it surpasses all human understanding. You must rise up from the natural to a great supernatural level of faith. I will thank Him for all eternity for my great gift of faith and love of the Holy Eucharist.

John 53

Jesus said to them, "Amen, amen,
I say to you, unless you eat the flesh
of the Son of Man and drink his blood,
you do not have life within you."

TWENTY-SEVEN

The Flowers of Saint Francis

One special evening in the middle '90s, I decided to go to a prayer and Rosary meeting in Riverside, led by Fr. Ike La Pueblo from Saint Christopher Catholic Church in Moreno Valley California. I was so blessed to meet other Catholics, but one in particular would remain present in my life for many years to come. Her name was Mickie. She was a petite woman from the Dominican Republic, and she made the evening very memorable. We knew we would remain sisters in Christ forever.

Time went on and I learned that Mickie was born in a car on her way to a Catholic hospital in the Dominican Republic. Her father was in the back seat assisting his wife while the neighbor drove like crazy. When they arrived at the hospital, the nuns greeted them in front of the hospital and exclaimed, "She is a miracle!" Thus, Mickie was named "Milagros" meaning Miracles, and I am sure there were many occurring in the car that day. She is a little person with a huge heart and a great faith.

Through the years, we experienced many adventures together. We began to travel, going two by two, and I discovered race car drivers can come in small packages. After all, she was

245

born in a car, racing to the hospital. I've always been kind of a cautious and average driver, but this little thing drove fast. When we'd make a pilgrimage to Santa Maria to retreats, she would move around those curves in the road pretty quickly, and I would hold on wondering why I couldn't just take a horse and buggy up there instead. I was known as a grandma driver in my family long before I ever became a grandma. So I just bowed my head and prayed while she drove. We loved traveling and praying together. Our friendship grew and grew and we saw and heard many miraculous happenings throughout the years.

Mickie, 3rd Order Franciscan

I joined a class at St. Mel Catholic Church in Norco, California, in October of 1998 to take a course called the *Basic Catholic Theology Course* and invited Mickie to come along with me. She was thrilled. This class was a 35-week course under the direction of Catholic evangelist Victor Claveau, who did a great job as facilitator. The course was both video by Dr. Scott Hahn, as well as text by Dr. Hahn, under the approval of Rev. Timothy Jernejcic, Parochial Administrator. We graduated with a diploma of achievement.

Every week on the drive to class, I would pray the Seven Sorrows Rosary along with a cassette tape by the gifted miracle priest, Father Peter Rookey, O.S.M. I was very blessed praying with Our Blessed Mother en route to these classes. The course was wonderful and the bonding between Mickie and I grew during those months. She became a very special part of my life. Jesus sent his apostles out two-by-two, and Mickie and I quickly came to learn the benefit of this type of discipleship.

During the course, we studied Sacred Scripture, the Magisterium, Salvation History, Common Objections, The Sacraments, and Living a Sacramental Life. There was a lot of fellowship after class with other students. Some evenings, we would stand in the parking lot until very late, praying together. The Holy Spirit was very powerful in those parking lot prayer gatherings. We were experiencing an early Church type of discovery, and we became a close-knit group, enjoying the journey of this class.

After all, it was a half year course and lots of content was covered. We were learning our faith, from a biblical perspective, and spreading it out to others. I could hardly wait for the next class each week. We would be so much stronger as Catholic Christians if every Catholic could take a theology course like this in order to gain a better comprehension of their faith. As I mentioned it was called the *Basic Catholic Theology Course*, but I can attest that while studying this course, Dr. Hahn was giving us far more than Catholic 101. My teachings early on in my great conversion were very mystical in essence, but these classes gave me the theological foundation of the faith. I was becoming a Catholic who could answer objections to our faith with Biblical proof text, along with reason and clarity.

After the wonderful experience of completing this course, Mickie and I would only see each other occasionally, but the bonding was there for life. Mickie was a Eucharistic minister at her Church. One day at Mass, she was deep in prayer, and she silently told the Lord, "I love, Teresa, so much. I want to be her sister."

And she heard His voice within her clearly respond to her prayer, "Have her drink from My cup." She cried as she felt blessed beyond measure. She understood His words to mean that we would be sisters in His precious Blood - "Blood Sisters." She called me and told me about it, but then the weeks went by and time passed without us pursuing it any further.

A few months later, I was in her local area and made a decision to go to Mass at her Church, which I had not done in years. I sat on the left side of the Church and unbeknownst to me, Mickie was the Eucharistic minister, even though it was not her scheduled day, someone had become ill so they asked Mickie to serve in their place. I looked up during Mass and there she was silently beckoning me to come up to her. When I saw her, I knew I had to go to her. She had the chalice.

I normally receive the Lord in the Host only, knowing full well that I receive both the Body and Blood of Christ in the consecrated Host. The call of the Lord to go up to Mickie was very powerful, and so I did. I did it without any memory of her special words from Jesus months prior. I then fulfilled His desire. I drank His precious Blood from the cup Mickie offered to me and answered Mickie's prayer from weeks before. She later reminded me of her miraculous encounter with Jesus asking to be my sister. She saw me coming towards her and was filled with the joy of the Holy Spirit. She knew we were truly sisters forever. How beautiful the Lord is. We are literally all brothers and sisters in the Body of Christ.

Time passed, and one day Mickie called me and told me she was going to join the Third Order Franciscans. I was thrilled for her. Her prayerful, gentle spirit fit the order of Saint Francis. After time spent in formation, Mickie invited me to the celebration of her formal entry into the Lay Franciscan Order. I had an amazing series of events before the wonderful day came. I kept being prompted to study the origin and meaning of the Tau Cross, the Franciscan symbol. I just assumed that it was my insatiable desire to know everything about anything to do with the Lord. So I delved into history and was blessed beyond measure with my new knowledge regarding the Tau Cross.

In researching, I discovered that it was the last letter in the Hebrew alphabet and that Saint Francis not only used it in his writings, but signed it as his only signature. It is a uniquely-shaped T. Saint Francis painted it everywhere. It has been the Franciscan symbol among Franciscans of various denominations for centuries. Saint Francis held the Tau Cross to be a living symbol of his life – the sign of the Passover. Saint Francis received the stigmata on the 17th of September, on Mount Alverna bearing the marks of his crucified Lord; the Tau Cross would become a part of his habit and a total expression of his life. The Tau Cross is an integral part of the Secular Franciscan order and Mickie was about to enter that expression. I felt very honored to be invited to such a blessed celebration.

The Church filled up early with family and friends of the 20 some people about to take their vows. I ended up sitting next to some of Mickie's relatives who are Protestants. The seating was worked out by the Holy Spirit, so that I would be seated next to a person with one particular question on his mind. The Holy Spirit had a plan. Some people in the Church were praying, others quietly talking to one another long before it started.

I had my head bowed in prayer for the novitiate Franciscans when I heard a person quietly say to me, "Would you be able to explain to me what the Tau Cross symbol means?"

It happened to be one of Mickie's relatives. I was stunned since this was the very subject I had just been prompted to intensely study – how good our God is. This Protestant man got the short version of the Tau Cross history, but seemed very satisfied. He smiled and thanked me for the teaching. I had served the Lord in His desire to assist this man in his journey of faith. I knew the Holy Spirit was very pleased.

The time had come for these holy people to answer the call to be lay Franciscans. The service was magnificent, as it was serene, prayerful, and scriptural. I was deeply praying for all of them with my eyes closed, when my mind filled with a spectacular waterfall. The water flowed with a peace that surpasses my understanding. The falls ended into a lake that was as still as eternity. This internal scene in my mind's eye was that of a lake of glass.

I then saw gorgeous, large white flowers in the waters above the falls, slowly come to the falls, and one by one, they fell very gently into the waters, streaming downward towards their destiny of perfect communion. Many large flowers under a perfect Hand of Design. One by one, they would go over the falls and then eventually land and float like swans upon the still waters of the lake.

I was so anointed I surely did not count the flowers, but later smiled with the thought that there must have been the same number of flowers as novitiates, answering the Franciscan call that day. The flowers were stunning, brilliant white, seeming to represent purified souls drifting under God's Domain. The scene was truly breathtaking. I felt as though I was very close to Heaven's landscape. All of this was going on through the vocational service. I floated through the entire afternoon and knew that this was a Body of Catholics raised to a very high supernatural level that afternoon which was pleasing to both Saint Francis of Assisi and Our Lord Jesus Christ.

Unexpected Glory!

Saint Francis of Assisi – pray for us.

I recently tried to find the flower and was led to the gardenia, and praise be to Jesus, that was the flower I saw that day. The gardenia; gorgeous with large soft beautiful petals and a heavenly fragrance; a flower to remember; a very special day to treasure. My sister Mickie, as beautiful as a gardenia.

Ezekiel 9:4

"... and the Lord said to him:
Pass through the city (through Jerusalem)
and mark an X on the foreheads of those
who moan and groan over all the abominations
that are practiced within it."
(The X was the Tau Cross)

TWENTY-EIGHT

Mirianna and Divine Mercy

On September 12th, 2005, the Feast Day of the Most Holy Name of The Blessed Virgin Mary, our little granddaughter, Mirianna, age sixteen months, fell into a fire pit in the Trinity Mountains in Northern California. The fire had been out for hours, but the coals beneath the white dust were red hot. She apparently toddled over and fell headfirst. As the baby struggled to get her head out of that incredible pain, using her hand and arm, her mother, standing a short distance away, ran to her cries. Her hand was melted, unrecognizable – this all happened within a matter of seconds.

She was flown by angel flight to Saint Francis Memorial Hospital in San Francisco. While in the air, the pilot told my daughter, Kimberly, all planes in the area had been alerted to allow Mirianna first position in the skies to get her priority flight to the hospital. The pilot said, "The skies are hers, Mrs. Ennis."

My daughter was lying in the plane with her baby almost unable to breathe from the suffering. She grasped onto the pilot's words with great hope looking at her darling Mirianna's melted arm and hand. Kimberly trusted that her prayers to the Lord were being heard and somehow knew that He was going to bring His Glory to this horrific situation.

Mirianna was admitted to the Saint Francis Burn Center and Kimberly would not leave the hospital for over a month. The Ennis family life would never be the same. At the time, Kimberly and Robert had five children. Robert stayed home to care for Mirianna's four siblings in Kimberly's absence, as he was always there to step into the breach and take care of the household when needed. There was no way Robert could work his outside job during this tragedy. Their great journey of faith would begin with enormous struggles ahead of them.

Mirianna's wounds required immediate and numerous surgeries. The doctor assigned to Mirianna was a renowned pediatric burn surgeon. He came to visit Kimberly the night before Mirianna's first surgery and solemnly informed her that there was a possibility he would have to amputate the hand and wrist. Mirianna had sustained second-degree burns on her head and severe third-degree burns upon her right hand, wrist and arm. Kimberly was beyond traumatized. She was still breast-feeding Mirianna, which would be a great blessing later on. Kimberly called me from the hospital after the doctor left her with the worst-case scenario news, and told me of this horrible event.

I sat there in shock trying to absorb the story, as calmly as possible for Kimberly's sake. After the call, when I told my husband, Dan, we both just sat there numb from the unbelievable news. We began planning my emergency flight to get to Kimberly and Mirianna as quickly as possible. As I packed my suitcase, I felt compelled to include a special magazine featuring an article on "The Divine Mercy Story of Stanley Villavicencio." I also packed Holy Water, a Rosary, Bible, and some very precious *Tears of Oil* I had received which were taken from a statue of the Blessed Mother.

I made the arrangements for Danny to manage the household for four days, while I was gone, including some dinners that I prepared ahead of time to make it easier on him. I have to say, I am the chief chef and bottle washer in our household. Dan really loves my cooking, and he misses it when I'm not around. I told Danny I would make him the most wonderful tacos ever, before I left. I wish I had that kind of energy today. I could run on five hours sleep any day of the week at age 58. The tacos we shared the night before I left were fantastic. I cleaned up, fed the dogs, and we went to bed around 9 p.m., as we had to get up at three a.m. in order to make the flight to San Francisco.

I awakened at around eleven p.m. and felt very sick to my stomach. I became very ill and vomited all night. I thought, Dear God, what was wrong with those tacos? Maybe it was the salsa, but my husband got up and said he felt fine. It wasn't the tacos, and so it began, one assault after another. Unbeknownst to me, a spiritual battle was beginning in an effort to prevent this grandmother from flying to her granddaughter to pray over her. It took all my strength that morning to get up, as the sick stomach kept me up all night.

When I got up, I prayed the Chaplet of Divine Mercy and packed the car to leave for the airport. I headed to Los Angeles International Airport very weak, praying the Rosary throughout the drive. I was on time and after boarding the plane and settling in, they announced over the P.A. system that there was trouble with the electrical on the plane, and we would be delayed for approximately two hours. I was stunned.

I prayed for God's Will to be done. The crucial first surgery on Mirianna's hand and arm was scheduled for eleven a.m., and I was going to be late. Oh, dear Jesus and Mary, help me. I want so much to be with my daughter to pray over the baby before she goes into surgery. Please, please Lord, answer my prayers. I offered it all to the Lord in the sufferings of Christ.

Electricians worked on the plane and we were San Francisco bound within two hours. After getting my luggage, I headed out to the craziness of all the people on the curbs of San Francisco airport trying to catch a taxi. One taxi driver pulled up appearing to be my ride, but was flagged by his boss to move up to the lady to the right of me and pick her up. This situation left me with a taxi driver that was actually planning on taking the lady on the right, as she had an expensive route and offered him a very large tip.

However, he got stuck with me and literally ordered me to put my own luggage in his trunk and then practically pushed me into the back of his taxi. I was horrified. I got in and he proceeded to curse and swerve all over the freeway and I began to softly cry. He had wanted to drive the other lady and was furious that he ended up with me and my short fare. He was yelling that his business was failing and I ruined his opportunity to gain substantial cash that day.

He was of Middle Eastern descent and I had trouble understanding what he was yelling at me, which was probably a blessing. I was so sick from not sleeping all night with the terrible nausea and vomiting and then felt like I had been thrown into a taxi torture machine in that nauseous condition.

I called the Holy Spirit into that taxi and began to pray my heart out for this man. I prayed for the Lord to cast out all spirits not of Him and begged Jesus to help this poor man in his sufferings. Then I began to pray out loud and reached out my arms over him and prayed with all the love possible for someone about to kill me. He was threatening to crash the taxi! He saw me praying over him in his mirror and began to calm down. His disbelief of my love was evident.

I prayed out loud for God to help him in his financial crisis and bring him many big tippers. I prayed for the Lord to bless him abundantly, and hold him up in his personal distress. A Holy Calm entered our taxi. God was extremely present and I knew the Holy Spirit had subdued the out-of-control driver, as only He can do. He slowed down, quit swerving and stopped cursing. God had calmed the storm. It was over. I arrived at the hospital very late and turned to him and handed him a twenty dollar bill for a tip. I told him that was all I could do and how sorry I was that he lost his "big profit" ride. I told him I would continue to pray for him and he stood there in shock. I saw tears in his eyes and he smiled and gave me a gentle hug and left.

At the hospital front desk, I submitted my driver's license for clearance to enter the private burn unit which was on the top floor. I literally ran through the hospital hallways dragging my rolling luggage and lugging a back pack in order to get to my daughter. When we saw each other we hugged so tightly, and she shared with me that the surgery had been postponed three hours and that we could go in and still pray over Mirianna.

The Lord put it all on hold, so I could pray with Kimberly over my granddaughter. God was way ahead of all my struggles. He is a very loving Father who protects us and answers our prayers. His Will is sovereign and great. We prayed for the surgeons, nurses, and the surgery. We prayed over our baby girl, pleading for the Divine Mercy of the Lord to be powerfully present in the operating room and we begged Our Blessed Mother to hold and care for our precious little darling in all of it. I made the Sign of the Cross on her burned arm, hand and forehead, over and over, anointing her with the *Tears of Oil* on a cotton ball.

The surgeons came in with a team to take Mirianna to surgery. Kimberly and I followed the gurney to the operating doors pleading with God to save her hand and arm, praying the

Memorare to Our Blessed Mother for protection as she went off to surgery. I had made it on time, His Time. I got to stand there and hold and comfort my anguished daughter, after all. Oh, how I love you Lord.

The surgery took place on September 15, the Feast Day of Our Lady of Sorrows. Many hours later the doctors and surgical team came out of the operating room with smiles on their faces to assure us the surgery was successful. They saved her hand. The doctor explained she would need a number of skin graft surgeries and follow-up reconstruction, but Mirianna would have her hand.

When evening came, I collapsed in my hotel room and fell deep asleep from exhaustion. I awakened the next morning around six to pray. After prayer, I remembered the Divine Mercy magazine I had packed with the great article of Stanley Villavicencio's story. It detailed his great encounter with the Lord when he died, and Jesus commanded him to spread the Divine Mercy message and Chaplet. Oh, how I love Stanley's miracle.

I had been prompted to pray the Chaplet for many years at three in the morning and three in the afternoon. I sat down on the hotel bed and opened up the magazine to the Stanley's article and nearly fell over on the bed from the heavenly scent of roses coming up from the pages filling the hotel room. Praise Be Jesus Christ! I knew that Our Lord of Mercy was with us and Mirianna would overcome this tragedy.

Excitedly, I packed up my little rolling suitcase with the magazine anxious to tell Kimberly what had just happened to me.

The walk to the hospital was hilly and exhausting, but my steps were filled with joy from the miracle of the roses. Once at the hospital, I raced to Mirianna's room and I began tell Kimberly about the magazine.

Kimberly cut me off, "Oh, Mom, not right now, this room is teeming with nurses in and out and I cannot concentrate. Please tell me later."

I replied, "O.K. honey, I will."

I sat with Kimberly and Mirianna just loving them, silently praying and assisting them in any way I could throughout the day. Much later in the afternoon Kim said, "Mom, I would love to hear about the magazine story now."

"Wonderful, Kimberly," I softly replied, as I sat down on the hospital bed with her, Mirianna and the magazine. When I opened it to Stanley's story, a very profuse rose scent came up again, permeating the hospital room - blessing Grandmother, daughter and granddaughter with a profound miracle. Three generations blessed by His Divine Mercy.

Unexpected Glory!

"My God, Kimberly, the Lord is with you, and Mirianna. Trust Him with all your heart, and He will direct your path."

We sat there silently thanking the Lord Jesus and The Blessed Mother for the Miracle of the Roses. Kim sat on the bed holding her baby with tears silently streaming from her eyes. We knew that no matter what was ahead of us, the Lord would bless the baby in all of it. His Peace was with us. Our Lady and her court would watch over Mirianna.

Dr. Judy Burns, a pediatrician attending a conference at the hospital during Kimberly's last weekend, lived near Kimberly in the Eureka area. It was God's handiwork that these two women would encounter one another the weekend before Mirianna was to be released. Dr. Burns offered to drive Kim and Mirianna home which is a 7-hour drive that Robert would not have to struggle to arrange. Dr. Burns generously bought Mirianna a brand new car seat for their journey home. She was great company for Kim on the drive home, and to this day, Judy and her husband, Arthur, are two of Kimberly and Robert's dearest friends. They have been a fantastic support in their lives. What a great blessing the friendship has been to all of them.

As the years have gone by, Mirianna has endured nine more surgeries, many of them requiring skin grafting from other parts of her body. Some surgeries were performed closer to our home in Southern California, at the renowned Grossman Burn Center in Santa Ana, CA. While at the Grossman Burn Center, my sister Linda lived only minutes away from their location. She would come to see Mirianna, her Goddaughter, at various times during her surgeries and bring Kimberly comfort and relief, and pray over her Goddaughter.

Mirianna stayed briefly at our home in Winchester, CA, during her recovery from the Grossman Burn Center surgeries. Her environment had to be very clean and there were great efforts to protect her from any infection. Battles were being fought on many levels – sleepless nights, lost work and money troubles were experienced by my daughter, and her husband, who was diligently working to keep everything going at their home up in Trinidad during Mirianna's recovery in Southern California. Their indomitable faith carried them through it all. There was an abundance of foot soldiers all over the country praying for Mirianna's recovery. Countless Rosaries, Chaplets of Divine Mercy, and Holy Masses were offered up for Mirianna throughout the years.

I would go before Jesus in the Blessed Sacrament and hold up my hand, wiggling and stretching my fingers pleading with Him to give Mirianna the same mobility. Kimberly and Robert would take turns walking the baby as she suffered in agony after each surgery, and they never lost hope in their exhaustion through each cross. Through the years, Mirianna recovered beautifully. God answered all the prayers and her recovery was miraculous.

Mirianna Butterfly, her middle name reflecting the Resurrection, was born during Easter season and would grow into a highly energetic, bright child. She is inquisitive and highly gifted, and she is also ambidextrous. The first time I saw Mirianna's drawings I was stunned to find out she could sketch or paint with either hand so artistically. She has been doubly blessed. She plays the harp primarily with her injured hand, and the harp is her musical instrument of choice – she loves playing it. What a miracle.

Her favorite past time during recess at school was the monkey bars; what better therapy for her hand? We called her "our little monkey." She really loves to pray, and she is a spiritually sensitive prayer partner. She goes out with her sisters in the front of their house to a big tree with a statue of the Madonna sitting under it, and kneels down to pray the Rosary with them. The Lord has given Mirianna many unique gifts, but the greatest one of all is her loving, compassionate heart. She will be a great role model some day for burn victims, a role model of hope. Thank you and Praise You Jesus of Divine Mercy. Jesus, We Trust in You.

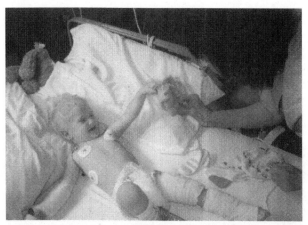

Mirianna's first series of surgeries.

One of her many skin grafts; always joyful.

Mirianna playing in a concert.

2013 My daughter, Kimberly, and her beautiful family at home in Northern California. From left to right: Mirianna Butterfly; Chiara Therese; Malachi Daniel Freedom (holding John Paul Maximilian); husband Robert Carl (holding Caelum Joseph Rain); daughter Kimberly Ann; Kephas Cathal; Lily Pearl; Kateri Rosemary; and Josiah SunRay.

Psalm 43:4

Then will I go into the altar of God,
the God of my gladness and joy,
Then will I give you thanks upon the harp,
Oh God, my God!

TWENTY-NINE

Something Beautiful for God

When we came back from our carnie escapades, I began to go to retreats and it was like finding pearls in a shell. I had never experienced that kind of fellowship with hundreds of people who were all of the same heart and mind. Perfect strangers would just stop and begin talking to you about the Lord and Our Blessed Mother and the joy and miracles they were experiencing in their lives.

In 1993, when I went to my first retreat in Santa Maria to meet Ron and Judy, many people came to speak and share their testimonies. Oh, those were the days of fantastic testimonies. Retreats were exploding all over the world with the power of the Holy Spirit and the faith level was very high. I was intensely enjoying everyone's conversion story. A significant conversion story I want to share is Michael Brown's, who would later host *Spirit Daily* on the internet.

I believe this was the year, in which I heard Michael Brown testify to the existence of Satan and the great magnificent power from Almighty God that works through Saint Michael the Archangel in the battle against evil. He stood up and gave his testimony about a tremendous series of dreams he had in his apartment and how his soul was saved and changed by visits from St. Michael. In those visits, St. Michael commanded him to order Satan away from his presence. At that time, he was investigating stories on gangsters and ghosts.

This testimony is recounted in his book, "*Prayer of the Warrior*," but I am reflecting on my personal experience with him in Santa Maria. I did not know anything about Michael Brown when I first heard him speak on this notable day in the '90s, but that was about to change.

Michael Brown stood in front of 300 plus people with the greatest humility and sincerity sharing his conversion story. I distinctly remember his closing, "I love all of you, (pause) and thank you for listening to my story."

I said to myself, "We love you, too, Michael. Your testimony was fantastic."

I remember being deeply inspired by the Holy Spirit during his talk and hoped I would get to hear him again someday. I could never have imagined what the Holy Spirit was doing with Michael Brown when he spoke that day in Santa Maria. His brush with demons and angels ignited his extreme flame of love, with which he was to later share in his books with others, about the Lord's passionate love to save us all.

Through the years, I would see Michael at various retreats in California and Florida. I found his retreats to be spiritually moving and vastly informative. I had a little money in those days and could get out and go to speaker-type retreats, prayer groups, and Bible classes. One evening in the '90s, Michael came to Brea, California area (I believe) and I was invited by a Goddaughter to attend this event.

During his talk, Michael asked the audience a question. "How many of you are being awakened at 3:00 a.m. in order to pray the Chaplet of Divine Mercy?" As I was raising my hand, I was stunned to look around the room to find every person holding up theirs. Michael then said, "Ah, you see the Holy Spirit is working through all of us the same way. We're all being called by the Lord to pray for our families and those around us in the great Chaplet from St. Faustina."

After the talk, he walked over and sat down next to me and began to share his trip to California. It was an unusual encounter, almost as though the Holy Spirit sat him down right next to me with purpose.

Then, out of the blue, he looked at me and said, "Are you having mystical spiritual experiences?"

I hesitated a moment, set back a bit from the question, and thought I should share a few of my spiritual experiences when someone joined us by sitting down right in between us. They started chatting with Michael, so I remained silent and our moment went away. I later thought that the Holy Spirit had given him a great gift of Holy discernment and word of knowledge particular to his type of work that was very powerful.

I would never have dreamed in the '90s that the day could come when I would not have money to travel nor the freedom to do so for various reasons. Traveling to Betania, Venezuela has been my only international trip, as I have been unable to go to Fatima, Lourdes, Medjugorje or Guadalupe, Mexico. In 1997, I began to read Michael Brown's, "Spirit Daily" as often as possible. I remember thinking about the articles throughout my work day and I could hardly wait for nighttime when I could read the next issue.

In those days, I worked a lot of hours, so I did not read his daily paper often, but when I did I would thank the Lord for such a great spiritual newspaper available for all to read. By 2001, my schedule calmed, and I was able to read it almost daily. I could not believe the amount of knowledge he was imparting to the world and to me – about spiritual happenings, saints, prophecies, angels, Church events, Blessed Mother Teresa of Calcutta and Saint John Paul II, politics, science, NDEs and everything in between. Oh, the ink and the paper that was flying off my printer almost daily was costly, and I found I did not want to part with any of it.

As you may recall, in 2001 I moved to a very remote piece of property in the desert and dedicated my days to my husband who had become wheelchair bound. Spirit Daily gave me the connection to every happening in the Catholic world and in the world period, therefore I was never lonely. Michael Brown brought me great joy, knowledge and unbeknownst to him, a sense of personal retreat almost daily without having to leave my driveway. Spirit Daily grew and grew through the years in the Holy Spirit and Wisdom.

I was having many spiritual experiences of my own and felt surrounded by a gigantic company of angels, saints and friends in my own cloistered setting that brought me a great deal of comfort. Kimberly, Robert, and all my grandchildren had to relocate to Northern California, near the Oregon border. Once they left, I was pretty much walking alone once again, just after moving to the desert with my husband. I missed them all tremendously. Spirit Daily, along with my prayer life, brought me a deep sense of belonging to God in His angels and saints.

Dan complained a lot about the paper and ink being used to print the Spirit Daily News. I must admit my passion was to print and read my articles at night with my head on my pillow. I looked forward to that short read before falling asleep each night – I guess it's reminiscent of my mom reading me bedtime stories – certainly more feasible than reading an entire book in an evening.

One morning as Dan and I were on our way to Mass, I began sharing that I had decided to do some cleaning in my prayer room, clearing out clutter and papers, and I found it was a sore subject and would soon regret mentioning it. He began to nitpick the topic of printing the Spirit Daily papers to shreds because of the ink. I was rather depressed by the whole conversation. I thought to myself, "I know honey, but after all, it is my daily connection to the outside Christian Catholic World that *I love so much.*"

I had regrets in bringing it up. I sure had wished we were discussing a topic like the Bible and the Lord on the way to Holy Mass. Well, by the time we arrived at Church I had completely forgotten all about it, and was looking forward to entering Heaven on Earth. That particular Sunday the reading from the book of Hebrews was all about hoping for things not seen, a living faith. Abraham had a living faith acted out in complete obedience to the Lord.

The gospel reading was Luke 12:32, speaking about "where your treasure is, there also will your heart be." The Pastor at that time, was Father Tony from Portugal, a very good, holy priest. His homily was particularly inspiring on the teachings of God in His Word and of the things to come for all of us. I was really soaking in all the scripture from the Holy Bible and the homily. Father Tony even quoted Pastor Billy Graham's famous saying, "I've never seen a U-haul trailer behind a hearse at a funeral."

I'm telling you – the readings, the gospel, the homily, the sense of being surrounded by saints and angels was overwhelming for me. I felt that wonderful lifting up of the soul that is indescribable.

As the homily was coming to end, with my eyes closed, I suddenly had the sensation and an acute visual field of being spiritually transported to a place of soft misty white fog in another dimension. I was running in slow motion with a great big smile with my arms outstretched. I was moving towards a being that was slowly materializing right in front of me. He was in a heavenly white gown, with long black hair, and a gorgeous smile with dazzling white teeth, without precise definition in His face. His arms were outstretched to receive me with great love, and I ran to Him. His Hands were covered in Spirit Daily papers and He was surrounded by them. They were beneath him, and all around him. The Lord Jesus had manifested in front of me with hair, hands, brilliant smile, dazzling white gown and Spirit Daily papers as His choice of sharing with me that beautiful morning. Then Jesus spoke to me with a huge smile in His illustrious style of communicating, "They are all about Me."

Unexpected Glory.

He infused knowledge that He was very pleased with my primary interest in reading all those hundreds of articles because the ones I favored the most were all about HIM. I began to cry profusely throughout the Consecration, Holy Eucharist and all the way to the end of Mass, when I could finally gain some composure. Thank, God, I always carry a roll of toilet paper to Mass in my purse. Kleenex would never handle the job. On the way home I just could not keep it to myself.

So I looked at Dan in the car and said, "Danny, Jesus told me during Mass that He likes the Spirit Daily papers."

My husband looked at me perplexed, but kindly said with a smile, "Well, honey, whatever you say." He seemed to have softened on the topic after the Mass. I wondered if Jesus had something to do with it?

A hush fell over the car after that brief discussion. Some things just cannot be conveyed to another unless they too have the encounter, but I pray this wonderful experience brings all of you joy. We are so blessed to have Spirit Daily, as Jesus Christ is so pleased with the articles about His Word, Grace, Mercy, Miracles, Faith, Knowledge, Our Holy Father and the Church. It inspires us all to pray for those that suffer or are in trouble. It reminds us of special events coming and brings news that we otherwise could not get. I continue to think of that revelation from Christ Jesus to this day. His smile. His approval. I live in the hope that I will see it again someday.

www.spiritdaily.com

Matthew 5:16

Just so, your light must shine before others,
that they may see your good deeds and
glorify your heavenly Father.

THIRTY

Forgiveness – the Key to God's Heart

Back in the '80s, I would occasionally attend a church in Riverside with my daughter, Kimberly, long before the "Miracle at the Truck Stop." I had no clue that you were supposed to go to Mass every Sunday. I can't really tell you why. I lived my adult life the way I was brought up. You went to church when it was convenient. Setting aside Sundays to worship God was just not at the top of my list yet. However, at this juncture in my life, I was beginning to feel a stronger desire to take my daughter Kimberly to Mass more regularly. I had an innate desire to go, even though, at that time, my husband was not a Sunday church-goer.

By now, my son Jeff was already grown and it was too late to take him along. He had only been to Mass occasionally as a child, with very little mention of God in our home. His adult life would reflect that later in a tragic way, that would bring great suffering to him and all of those around him, most particularly me, as his mother, but taking my daughter occasionally was a great joy for me. I had always been responsible, taking Kimberly and my son to Catechism, as I did love the Lord, but in a shallow sort of way. I did not intimately know Him, not yet anyway.

The nuns planted powerful "Seeds of Glory" in my early childhood, but there was no one to nurture those seeds through my teen and early adult years. Nevertheless, God reads hearts and has always known my intentions. He formed me in my mother's womb, had always known my heart and where it was heading. His call on me was getting stronger, even before I personally met Him at the truck stop. I was beginning to respond, even though I was walking this road completely alone.

I enjoyed Mass occasionally at a large cathedral-type church, but really did not develop a relationship with any priest there during that period of time. Kimberly was confirmed at that church, but no strong pastoral connection had been made. I remember how much I desired to be an active parishioner of that church and be involved, but just could not get my husband or son to go. I was attending Mass there, without being a participate in the Church community.

As the years flew by, my dad Raymond got very ill. His heart was failing and after a few weeks in the hospital, I knew that our time with him was short. I got on my knees in the hospital one afternoon and took dad's hand in mine and told him how much I loved him. With many tears flowing, I told him that I was so sorry for any trouble I brought into his life when I was a teenager and hoped that I had made it all up to him through the years. He just kept nodding yes, yes, yes. The love passing back and forth between us was tremendous in that hospital room.

He was not able to talk anymore, but he could shake his head and show understanding in his eyes. I suddenly regretted all the moments I could have sat and asked him questions about his life and didn't. He was a very quiet man. Oh, how we can let precious moments slip away from us.

The next day my mother began to call all the family to come and be with her and dad, a wonderful husband and father of forty years. Aunts, uncles, cousins, grandchildren, everyone came. Mother knew that time was short. I had a very strong call on my heart to get a priest to come to the hospital and pray the Sacrament of Extreme Unction, today known as Anointing of the Sick (Last Rites), upon my father. I went to find my mother in the hospital to let her know what I was about to do.

She was very, very upset. "Oh, no, you can't bring a priest in there, you will scare your father."

"Mom, he will not be scared, he will be blessed."

I had no idea why she was acting like that, and would not understand it for many, many years. Nonetheless, I was not daunted by her strong admonition. It was a blueprint of how I had been raised. Although, I never witnessed my dad going to Confession or Holy Communion, however he would occasionally take us to Mass. There seemingly was some sort of stumbling block in their marriage for them to partake in the Sacraments, but I still felt that the Last Rites were necessary at the end of my dad's journey.

I did not analyze the situation, I simply acted without knowledge, strictly from the heart. I had never questioned why he did not participate in the sacraments himself, but he took me to confession and sat outside in his car. You just did not ask your parents personal questions in those days. You did not question them period.

I left the hospital and drove over to the Church and knocked on the rectory door. Another visitor walked up and also waited with me, so when the door opened, I stepped back and let her speak to the priest first. I did not know the priest, but remembered that over the years, he celebrated some Masses I attended. I didn't go very often, so I was not a familiar face to him. He did not know me from Adam. He was rather brusque in his response to the other visitor and she left.

There I was, standing in front of him, with the Lord Jesus, The Blessed Virgin and the angels. "Hi, Father, my dad is gravely ill, he is at the Riverside Community Hospital and I was wondering, could you come and give him the Last Rites sometime today?"

He shot back at me, "That's not going to save him. I'm too busy. Get someone else."

Then he slammed the door in my face. I stood there and could feel the tears stinging my cheeks. I had to gather my composure in order to drive back to the hospital. I was so perplexed and hurt at the priest's behavior, but I was prompted to go forward with hope and perseverance. I later found out his name was Father Jim.

I went back to the hospital and asked the desk clerk if there was Catholic clergy in the hospital and she said, "Yes. The priest will be back after 4 p.m."

So she contacted the hospital priest and made a date for 7 p.m. that evening in my dad's hospital room. My mother accepted it and would later realize what a divine appointment it would prove to be. My mother, husband, daughter, sisters, all the relatives and even my son came in the room when the joy-filled Asian priest arrived.

He gave my father the Last Rites and then asked us all if we would pray the Rosary with him for my father. I will never forget it. I had a knowing that my dad heard every word. Every relative; those that had left the Church, those that had gone to other churches, those in no church at all, knelt down to participate. The Holy Spirit permeated the entire hospital room with a Cloud of Love in the "Bible on a String" prayers of the Holy Rosary. The anointing of the sick became the anointing of my whole family.

My dad's end of life here, was blessing everyone in their lives at that moment. When it was over, the relatives all left and my husband took all the kids to our house to allow my mother and a few of us alone time with him. My beloved sisters, Kathryn and Linda, my son Jeff, and, Aleta, a dear woman who lived as a part of our family for years – all joined my mother as we prayed for the rest of the night.

At approximately 3 a.m., my mother completely yielded to the Holy Spirit and said, "I release you Raymond to go to God. Lord, please take him."

She was crying her eyes out. My Dad passed away immediately, upon her giving her husband back to the Lord, and we all felt his spirit come up around us.

I accepted everything, but understood nothing, but this I did know – that me and my sisters loved our parents immensely and this loss was overwhelming to us. Mother and her daughters began to make arrangements for a funeral Mass. Mother very much wanted the Catholic Funeral Mass for dad. It was that mix of some things Catholic, but not all things Catholic in our lives. My husband Dan was one of the greatest supports for mother in all the preparations, as I was too weak. Dan was the faithful son-in-law to my parents to the very end. He was always very good and kind to my parents. They grew to love him as their very own son.

Twenty-four years later, when my mother was getting ready to pass away, she raised up in her hospital bed, when she thought she saw a priest, and said, "I want to confess."

The desire to repent was so strong in her, and in the end, my mother had truly become a Catholic in her heart. All fear and concerns about scandals in the Church, fell away from my mother at that moment. She knew that only the Catholic Church had the authority to absolve sin and, in the end, she pleaded for confession.

Time passed by and I would think about that priest shutting the rectory door on me and I began to forgive him. Years later, after the truck stop miracle, I knew I had to pray a lot for that priest. I had a different approach to struggles with forgiveness. I was reading the Bible intently and understood the graces God gives us in those matters if we pray for it and allow Him to lead us. I grew to actually care about that priest in prayer. My deep conversion into the Catholic Church brought expectations from the Lord upon me, one being deep forgiveness in the heart for all those who betray or hurt us in any way.

One day, ten years after he slammed the door in my face, I woke up with a strong desire to go over to that same Church for Mass, as I was being prompted by the Holy Spirit to do so. I had never gone back to that Church after that incident – not by intent, but because I belonged to a totally different parish, many miles from that one. But this was a very strong prompting, so I got up and drove over there by myself. Remember, it had been ten years. I went in and began to pray right away. It was a wonderful feeling to be there again. It is a stunning cathedral-like Church.

Before Mass began, someone made an announcement that a visitor wanted to speak for a moment to all of us. I could not believe my eyes as it was the priest, the one that I had prayed for throughout the years, *the door slammer*, that went up to the podium and began to speak. "Good Morning to all of you. My name is Fr. Jim. Many years ago I was a parish priest here. I have been gone for almost ten years. I have returned today to humbly beg the forgiveness of anyone I may have ever hurt, been rude to, or caused their faith to falter in any way. You see, I am an alcoholic. I was drinking in those days and I know that I left behind some damage here. I have come to apologize to anyone I may have crossed paths with when I was drinking or expressing alcoholic behavior towards them, while at this Church. Please forgive me!"

The Lord drew both of us back to that Church on that particular morning for Father Jim's public confession to all the parishioners, at that exact hour, so that I could experience the fruits of forgiveness.

Unexpected Glory.

I thought I would fall over in the pew. I witnessed profound humility and courage from this priest emboldened by the Holy Spirit. I can still recall in great detail the way he spoke to me and made me feel during a time of such tremendous personal loss. I then deeply understood why he had acted the way he did the morning I knocked on his door. *Forgiveness.*

What a wonderful gift from the Holy Spirit. All I could feel for this priest was great love, watching him speak in front of that huge congregation, begging for forgiveness for his past actions. What a great privilege to be called there that morning. He then told us that he was the resident priest at a drug and alcohol treatment home which had been his address for quite a while. It is impossible to describe the joy I felt, that the Lord would knit us together that morning in such a miraculous way.

A few months later I went to the rehab house and asked to see him. He was there and welcomed me into his little home with open arms. I could tell he did not remember me at all from the incident years earlier. He offered me a cup of coffee and I began to tell him all about my son. I shared my son's childhood and his addiction problem with this now, very loving priest.

When we were all done he stood up, gave me a hug and told me he would include my son, Jeff, in every morning Mass he said in his private chambers. What a gift. Only God can do such magnificent things in our lives. The Lord turns lemons into lemonade for those who love Him and patiently wait for Him to answer prayers, and those answers are not always what we expect or as timely as we would like. I know that even now, twenty years later, I feel so much love for that priest. I pray we cross paths in eternity so I can give him a loving embrace and share every detail of the whole story. Will he ever be surprised when he and I relive that scene in our eternal home, standing at that rectory door that morning so many years before, however the Lord decides to share this with the both of us when we leave here, and we will jump for joy in heaven and celebrate God's Mercy together.

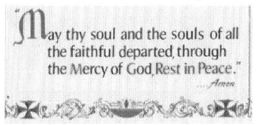
"May thy soul and the souls of all the faithful departed, through the Mercy of God, Rest in Peace."
...Amen

Colossians 3:12, 13

Put on then, as God's chosen ones,
holy and beloved, heartfelt compassion,
kindness, humility, gentleness, and patience,
bearing with one another and forgiving one another,
if one has a grievance against another;
as the Lord has forgiven you, so must you also do.

THIRTY-ONE

Priests for Lifers

If we as Catholics are open to it, priests are with us for life – from womb to the tomb. As a person who is committed to her faith, I guess I would call myself a Catholic Lifer. The office of Holy Orders (priests) will always be there. Your local priest might move, but you'll always have the priesthood.

The day I was born, May 14th, 1948, Israel became a state and declared independence. During that year many major events were happening all around the world. Mother Teresa was entering her beloved Loreto Convent to pray, suffer and work with the poorest of the poor for the rest of her life. Wonderful Father Patrick Peyton was forming, "The Family Rosary Crusades" that would emanate globally, *"The family that prays together, stays together."* Excavations for the Tomb of St. Peter under the Vatican were being noted in Life Magazine.

I was born on the heels of Stalin and Hitler and their tremendous anti-God forces against the world and the Catholic Church. Now they are just names in old dusty books lying in repose, scorned upon, in horror of their deeds. The war had ended – Praise God for His Mercy. We endlessly thank Our Lord for all the priests and nuns who served so selflessly throughout history at great personal sacrifice, even unto death.

The Cristiada movement and the Carmelite nuns, most especially Mother Maria Luisa Josefa, that fled from Mexico to California had greatly impacted the Los Angeles area schools beginning in the '30s and '40s. Mother Maria Louisa provided a refuge for many immigrants. She became a light in the darkness at great personal risk.

May 14th is also the feast day of St. Matthias in the Catholic Church, chosen by the apostles drawing lots after Judas hung himself in the Field of Blood. Twelve was the number reflecting the twelve tribes of Israel, and Judas had been chosen initially by Jesus Christ. As Catholics, we understand that this process by the apostles of choosing Matthias shows the Lord's desire of succession of bishops and the succession of bishops ever since – a permanent office. St Peter, Chief of the Bishops, would later become my hero.

How blessed we are to have an unbroken line of 266 Popes to reflect upon – a miracle in and of itself. Thank you, Almighty God, for Pope Francis. I came to believe in the Authority bestowed upon the Catholic Church by Jesus Christ himself and knew that the filling of Judas seat with a new Apostle, chosen by lot, St. Matthias, was providentially mandated by God. This conviction would explode in me 44 years after my awesome baptism. No media, no scandals, no one at all, could shake my faith in Jesus Christ and His Church. How blessed I am to be born on the Feast Day of St. Matthias which encouraged me to study the Office of Bishopric.

I was named after St. Teresa of something (I never knew which Teresa it was). St Theresa the Little Flower or St. Teresa of Avila – my parents never talked to me about it while I was growing up; but it's in my baby book (my personal history reference). It says, "This baby girl named after St. Teresa."

My parents never mentioned saints to me, so I'm guessing it was my grandmother Asunción who influenced my name. I did have a clue in the baby book because there was no "h" in the baby book and there is no "h" in my name, so I believe St. Teresa of Avila is my namesake, but I didn't want to hurt any feelings, so I adopted them both as my Patron Saints and I asked them to walk along side of me in my life. Two doctors of the Church; both of them magnificent Carmelites; both of them my namesakes; both of them a gift from God; and Teresa of Avila is the patron saint of Catholic writers which I just recently discovered.

Unexpected Glory.

As I reflect on the day my parents and grandparents (who are also my Godparents), carried me through the Church doors to be baptized at Saint Patrick's Catholic Church in Los Angeles, I raise my hands to praise and thank God for that moment in time.

Twenty-three years after my baptism, Reverend Julio Cancelli wrote me a beautiful letter and invited me back to the old Church before it was demolished because of extreme damage during the 1971 San Fernando earthquake. How he ever found me back in the days before personal computers is way beyond my comprehension. I send great gratitude for the truly love-filled letter he sent asking me to come and see the Church, and most particularly the baptismal font where I first became a Catholic Christian.

I can't help but wonder if that dear priest sent a letter like this to everyone that was in that Baptismal Register. It emanates the works of priests all over the world. He wanted me to see where I first became a Christian and was brought into the family of God. Unfortunately, I couldn't go because I had to work. I was a waitress in those days and it was difficult to miss a shift. In retrospect, I thank God for the Reverend's loving letter he wrote to me. Oh, how I wish I could have appreciated it more back then. I pray he can experience my gratitude from where ever he is now.

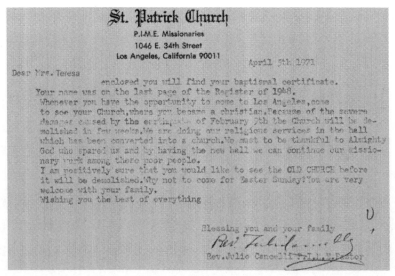

St. Patrick Church

P.I.M.E. Missionaries
1046 E. 34th Street
Los Angeles, California 90011

April 5th 1971

Dear Mrs. Teresa

enclosed you will find your baptismal certificate. Your name was on the last page of the Register of 1948. Whenever you have the opportunity to come to Los Angeles, come to see your Church, where you became a christian, because of the severe damages caused by the earthquake of February 9th the Church will be demolished in few weeks. We are doing our religious services in the hall which has been converted into a church. We must to be thankful to Almighty God who spared us and by having the new hall we can continue our missionary work among these poor people. I am positively sure that you would like to see the OLD CHURCH before it will be demolished. Why not to come for Easter Sunday? You are very welcome with your family. Wishing you the best of everything

Blessing you and your family

Rev. Julio Cancelli P.I.M.E. Pastor

I have such profound gladness in my heart to God for all the priests and nuns that have been present in my life. I want to share the greatness of their works through the Lord's Church that had a timeless effect in my heart in the seeds of glory they planted. What would the world do without them? Padre Pio said, "Better a day without the sun, than without the Eucharist."

Can we even comprehend how true that is? Do our priests comprehend the magnitude of that truth as well and how it affects us as parishioners? Their role in salvation history needs to be praised and recognized in today's modern world. They need to know how much they are loved and appreciated by all Catholic lifers. They are our life line in running the race, sacramental strength for our journey. It is their presence and what they represent, that brought me to where I am today.

My childhood was filled with memories of interaction with Monsignor Gallagher at St. Thomas Catholic School, including when he handed me the certificate of honor for exceptional reading of books. Watching them serve the Holy Mass throughout my life are imbedded visuals in my soul forever. The last words I want to hear when I leave this earth are, "The Body of Christ." I cry every time I hear it.

Only a priest can give me that sacrament. That is who I pray will be with me in the last moments of my life, besides my husband and family, of course. I thank God for the gift of being able to believe in my heart that the priest has the authority given him from Jesus to bless my life with the sacraments, rather than focusing on his individual weaknesses and character defects. Don't we all have them?

During great struggles in my family life, I remember being very distressed and going to priests for counsel. It has been very comforting to me, as their counsel was deeply spiritual and their guidance was directed by the Church. I received teachings on marriage in a condensed form from Catholic priests; teachings that have come down through the 2,000 years of Mother Church. Those sessions enlightened and strengthened me for my life's journey, especially my 49 years of marriage.

At one time in my life, I taught piano to children. I will never forget when I learned that notated music was constructed from Gregorian chant. Pope Gregory in the fifth century was gifted by God with much of the essence of that contribution. Music, schools, hospitals, charitable organizations, law (that came from Canon Law), free market economics and the profound respect for life from the womb to the tomb moved forward in history for 2,000 years throughout the Church. How blessed the world is that monastic religious are praying 24-hours a day for the world, nonstop.

When do you ever hear people talking about those religious and the graces that come from them? The list is endless and timeless, but it is rare to hear someone bring up the contributions made by the Catholic Church to humanity with loving praise. Take a moment and study St. Elizabeth Ann Seton, St. Kathryn Drexel and Fr. Junipero Serra. Their statues are surrounding the capital building in Sacramento, California. Sacramento is named after the sacraments. What a field trip it is to study the history of the 21 missions. Oftentimes, the media will permeate households with the dark side of our Church, seldom discussing the great works going on daily in the world by the Church. But for anyone in the Catholic Church, if you are really gleaning all she offers, your socks will be blessed off.

I love thinking about the monks penning the scriptures with candles before Edison ever came to light. My life has been saturated with the scriptures in Holy Mass as I hear the entire Bible about every three years on Sundays and every year if I attend daily Mass. The Scriptures really come to life on the altar. In the Mass, you move from the Old Testament reading and Psalms that bring about visuals of the Temple, the Torah, the yarmulke (beanie), menorahs, altars, chanting and manna. From there, we enter the New Testament which brings visuals of Cathedrals, the Bible, the zucchetto (beanie), liturgical candles, altars, singing and the Eucharist – from the Passover to the Eucharist. We are truly fed in the Catholic Church during the sacrifice of the Mass, with both the Liturgy of the Word and the Liturgy of the Eucharist. You are what you eat.

I hope that priests realize the importance of wearing their clergy clothing in public. The very image itself is representative of the Catholic Church and needs to be visible to all. Father, you have the mission to save souls, not only by what you do, but by the image you imprint in the eye of the beholder. I love to see clergy in their religious attire, resonating the word *Church* wherever they go.

Your image, in clerical attire, stays in the mind and soul of those who see you. The vestment colors communicate the liturgical seasons to everyone, such as red for Pentecost; violet for Lent, Sacrament of Reconciliation and Anointing of the Sick; green for Ordinary Time; White for Easter, Christmas and so many other Holy Days; to name a few.

I want to acknowledge with the greatest love, honor and respect our Holy Father, our Cardinals, Bishops, Priests, Nuns, Missionaries, Monks, Deacons and all those who work for the Lord in the Church. I want to mention very special priests and nuns who have been close to me in my life. Many of whom I have had private talks, retreats, gone to their classes, and received the sacraments from - oh, so very many. I have had an abundant outpouring of graces during the reception of the sacraments throughout my life that these religious never knew about. I have had some of my greatest miracles and revelations during Holy Mass of which some are shared in this book.

I thank the Great Lord for all of the religious in my life - from my birth all the way to my coming death on earth. *I love you all, wherever you are, with all my heart.* Priests for Lifers. Priests in every order in the world. May one of my nine grandchildren become a priest or a nun, if it be your will, dear God.

The following are priests who have greatly affected my life in a hundred different ways. I've had a special devotion of praying for aborted babies for years. I thank God for the Priests for Life Ministry whose work has saved so many babies. Also, for the many priests I never knew, who are doing work in remote parts of the world. I pray for them all. For all the martyred priests, even most recently in the Middle East and Africa, and all the military chaplains that have served so selflessly. May they too know how much they are loved. We need to pray for them faithfully and fervently.

For every nun, in her particular order, joyfully living her lifetime vows as a consecrated virgin. For every martyred nun, diocesan nun, missionary nun and cloistered nun, your prayers for the world rain down God's graces on to every corner of the Earth. I pray for all of you, always. I also pray you read this book and feel my deep gratitude for the religious. May the Lord bless you all mightily wherever you are in your journey.

The Great Religious in My Life

Rev. Pat Crowley, SSCC

Rev. John Hampsh, CMF

Rev. Frank Pavone

Rev. Mitch Pacwa, SJ

Rev. Jose Maniyangat

Rev. Michael Sears

Rev. Matthew Munoz

Rev. Jonathan Morris

Rev. Fr. Louis Marx

Rev. Michael Barry, SSCC

Rev. Petar Ljubicic

Rev. Ray Skonezny, STL, SSL

Rev. Wm. Casey, CPM

Rev. Atchley

Rev. Robert Spitzer, SJ, PhD

Msgr. Timothy Keeney

Rev. De Grandis

Rev. Gary Sumpter

Rev. Timothy Deeter

Rev. Edward Sousa, Jr.

Msgr. Ray Kirk

Msgr. James Lisante

Rev. Gene Sabio, MSC

Rev. Wm. Erstad

Rev. Tony Das Neves

Rev. John Struzzo, CSC

Rev. Donald Calloway, MIC

Rev. Joseph Whalen

Rev. Peter Rookey, OSM

Rev. Adrian Budhi, MSC

Rev. Julio Cancelli

Rev. John A. Hardon, SJ

Rev. Fred Costales, MS

Most Rev. Gerald Barnes

Saint Padre Pio

St. John Paul II

Pope Benedict XVI

Pope Francis

Msgr. Gallagher

Rev. Melvin Doucette

Rev. Dwight Longenecker

Rev. Maurice Cardinal, MS

Rev. Ike LaPuebla, Jr., MS

Rev. Jozo Zovko

Rev. Svetozar Kraljevic, OFM

Rev. Finbarr Devine

Rev. Patrick Peyton, CSC

Rev. Francis Gloudeman

Rev. Tom Burdick

Bishop del Riego

For every Carmelite who ever held me in their arms as a small babe, and for those who taught me how to pray and to love Jesus and Mary.

For The Immaculate Heart Sisters at St. Thomas School who gave me my incredible early Catholic education and began to truly form the discipline in my soul. The following is a list of the different Orders of Sisters who have had a great impact in my life:

Mother Maria Luisa Josefa

St. Teresa of Avila

Sister Lucia of Fatima

Sister Doloras

Sister Conception

Sister Rafael

Sister Emily

Mother Antonia

St. Therese of Lisieux

St. Faustina Kowalska

St. Frances Cabrini Sisters

Sister Mary De Sales

Sister Mary Bonaventure

Sister Briege McKenna

Sister Scholastica

St. Teresa Benedicta of the Cross

Sister Timothy Ann Marie

Sister Dolorosa

Immaculate Heart of Mary Sisters

I hope this book will be a spotlight of honor to shine His glory upon all religious, as Pope Francis has dedicated 2015 to be the Year of Consecrated Life.

Please pray for Pope Francis and all the religious.

Thank you, Lord, for my life in you and your Church.

Amen.

1 Corinthians 7:32-35

I should like you to be free of anxieties.
An unmarried man is anxious about the things
of the Lord, how he may please the Lord.
But a married man is anxious about the things
of the world, how he may please his wife,
and he is divided. An unmarried woman
or a virgin is anxious about the things
of the Lord, so that she may be holy
in both body and spirit.
A married woman on the other hand,
is anxious about the things of the world,
how she may please her husband.
I am telling you this for your own benefit,
not to impose a restraint upon you,
but for the sake of propriety and adherence
to the Lord without distraction.

EPILOGUE

Every soul on earth is loved by God. *Unexpected Glory* happens – every second. Look inward within yourself, look up, and be still in Him. He awaits your thoughts, your childlike love. The Lord blesses a contrite heart and a teachable spirit. He is our Creator, our Redeemer and our Sanctifier. His Mercy knows no boundaries. Every moment of your life is a potential encounter with God waiting to happen. Never think that God is not present in your life, no matter where you are at the moment. Your miracles are different than mine; they may be big, they may be small, visible or hidden. Some may be for others in your life, and some may be just for you.

Imagine, never spending any time with those you love? Never putting any effort into your relationships? Does your relationship with the Lord include moments replete with just loving Him? Do you turn to Him throughout the day like a child to a Father asking for His help and assistance? Do you completely depend upon His Grace and Mercy? Do you stop periodically in your busy day and tell Him you love Him? These are the potential moments of miracles in your life. Listen.

Unexpected Glory.

God is never unavailable. In sickness and in health, in war and peace, in riches and in poverty – God interacts with all of us in ways we cannot comprehend. His ear is always inclined to our lips.

We are all unique in creation. Be aware of God working in your life. He is awaiting your attention, love and trust. He is always with you. Tell him how much you love Him today. Tomorrow may never come.

Teresa with husband, Danny, of 49 years.

StJoesfarm(AT)AOL.com
707-296-5996 cell